T0372503

Urban Informal Settlements

Yannan Ding

Urban Informal Settlements

Chengzhongcun and Chinese Urbanism

Yannan Ding
Centre for Historical Geography Studies
Fudan University
Shanghai, China

ISBN 978-981-16-9201-7   ISBN 978-981-16-9202-4   (eBook)
https://doi.org/10.1007/978-981-16-9202-4

This Palgrave Macmillan imprint is published by the registered company Springer Nature Singapore Pte Ltd.
The registered company address is: 152 Beach Road, #21-01/04 Gateway East, Singapore 189721, Singapore

To My Parents

CONTENTS

LIST OF FIGURES

xii   LIST OF FIGURES

LIST OF TABLES

CHAPTER 1

Introduction

Abstract In this section of the book, I set forth the aim of the whole study by relating the *chengzhongcun* phenomenon in contemporary Chinese cities with its variegated predecessors, as well as urban informal settlements in other countries. In particular, the works of Herbert J. Gans serve as an important point of reference in discussing slum elimination efforts in two very different settings, namely post-war United States and pre-reform China. Moreover, the (re-)emergence of the *chengzhongcun* in post-reform China, especially the two decades since 2000, is re-embedded into the larger picture of global urbanisation, especially of the Global South. As the *chengzhongcun* gains attention from policy-makers and urban China scholars, China is making efforts to implement the Millennium Development Goals (MDGs). This chapter concludes by introducing the contents of the following chapters.

Keywords *Chengzhongcun* · Slum · Herbert J. Gans · Millennium Development Goals (MDGs) · Urban China

> *It can be argued that modern social geography began in the slums of nineteenth-century British cities.* (Pooley & Lawton, 1988: 159)

"There are nine million bicycles in Beijing. That's a fact. It's a thing we can't deny."[1]

Whether that statement is, or once was, true I am not sure. But what I am sure is that nowadays in China you can order a set of LEGO-style assembly blocks of the *chengzhongcun* and have it delievered at your doorstep by the next day. There are also online games with scenes setting in the *chengzhongcun*, and the numerous online discussion forum posts, video reportages, as well as research papers about it. People live with the *chengzhongcun* without necessarily live in it. In the city of Shenzhen, you could even have broadband package specially catered to the needs of *chengzhongcun* residents. It's rural, and yet urban. But what, after all, is a *chengzhongcun*?

To answer that question, we may travel back in time to the opening years of the 1960s, which arguably marked one of the lowest points of international relationships. The Sino-Soviet split revealed that the Communist sphere was anything but a seamless block, whereas the Cuban Missile Crisis was putting the world on the verge of nuclear warfare. The United States of America and the People's Republic of China were ideologically distantiated as much as it could be and, needless to say, there was no diplomatic relationship between them. Yet, there were two books published in New York and Shanghai respectively around the same time, viz. *The Urban Villagers: Group and Class in the Life of Italian-Americans* (Gans, 1962) and *The Transformation of Shanty Towns in Shanghai* [Pinyin: *Shanghai penghuqu de bianqian*] (Shanghai Academy of Social Sciences, 1962).

Herbert J. Gans, who would later become one of the iconic figures in American urban and cultural studies, not least because of his 1988 chairmanship of the American Sociological Association (ASA), was commissioned by the Harvard Medical School and the Massachusetts General Hospital to study a migrant community called the West End in Boston. This place name easily reminds one of a previous study on the North End in the very same city, *Street Corner Society: the Social Structure of an Italian Slum* (Whyte, 1943). William F. Whyte's influence on Gans was profound. Both of them focused on migrant communities, mainly of Italian descendants, and both had adopted participative observation as the key research method, etc. The young researcher Gans studied the

---

[1] Excerpts taken from the lyrics of Katie Melua's *Nine Million Bicycles*.

"nature and dynamics of working- and lower-class society and culture, and the impact of redevelopment and relocation" of the Italian American community, and published his first book, *The Urban Villagers*. But the situation had change between Whyte's time and his. For Gans, the 1949 Housing Act was the watershed (Gans, 2007: 232). In the United States, "urban renewal" as an idea came out only after the act, which was the precursor of the slum clearance movements in the 1950s. Meanwhile, post-war exodus from the city was made possible through the building of numerous suburban and low-density communities, one of which later appeared in the title of Gans' second book, *The Levittowners: Ways of Life and Politics in a New Suburban Community* (Gans, 1967).

On this side of the Pacific, the work collectively edited by the Urban Economics Group, Institute of Economic Studies, Shanghai Academy of Social Sciences was one of a series of pamphlets glorifying the achievements after the Communists' taking over of the city in 1949. The aim, as exemplified in the foreword, is to expose the miseries of the "Old Shanghai" as the bastion of both colonial exploitation and capitalist repression of the working people, many of whom were forced to living in shacks (Fig. 1.1). By contrast, since the early 1950s, the city had made great achievements through slum upgrading and resettlement projects.

The editors juxtaposed photographs of the plight of the people living in shacks before 1949 and the new boulevards or apartment buildings in the same sites after 1949. Many shanty towns had been demolished or at least reconstructed. It seemed that the pamphlet was a success and it was reissued in several versions, including a last one in 1971, changing its otherwise plain cover design into a drastic revolutionary style during the zenith of the "cultural revolution" (1966–1976). That was, as a matter of fact, the time when urban construction was stalling and tens of thousands of teenagers were dispersed into rural areas in the "down to the countryside movement" [Pinyin: *shangshan xiaxiang*]. But it was also a time when China and the United States were about to normalize their relationship. Richard M. Nixon set foot on Shanghai in February 1972 and changed the course of the Cold War.

Half a century later, China has transformed itself from a predominantly rural to an industrialized and urbanized nation. China was less than 20% urbanised in the late 1970s. The latest census shows that the figure has risen to more than 62% (Ning, 2021). The scale of the breath-taking urbanisation of China is unprecedented in human history. Cities grow in number, in size, and vertically in height. New business modes as well as

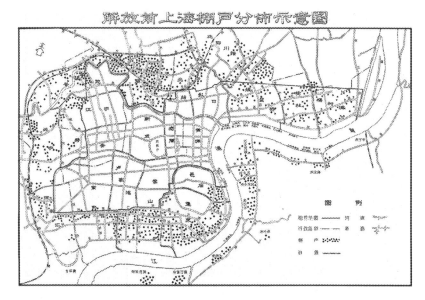

Fig. 1.1 Map of Shanty Town Distribution in Shanghai before the Liberation (*Source The Transformation of Shanty Towns in Shanghai,* 1962)

new cultural phenomena mushroomed in cities and towns across of the country. Urban space in China has been an incubator of a new kind of urbanism, many aspects of which have been examined over the last two decades (see: He & Wu, 2009; Wu, 2010; Douglass et al., 2012; Wu et al., 2014; Iossifova, 2015; Wong & Liu, 2017; Woodworth, 2018; Oakes, 2019; etc. for but a few examples).

It is, however, beyond the scope of this book to investigate the long and rich history of Chinese urbanism, or to formulate a comprehensive survey of contemporary urbanism in China. The focus will be set upon the urban fringe where the growth of the city is most visible. It is by no means to neglect urban growth taking place elsewhere, whether in the form of often outlying Economic and Technological Develop Zones (ETDZs) or inner city urban renewal projects. The emphasis on visibility is based on two observations. First and foremost, the urban fringe is not a specifically designated area, as in the case of the ETDZs, thus its boundary is open and largely permeable. Secondly, the urban fringe forms a sort of blendscape between the city and its other, which may not be simply described as rurality. If its social heterogeneity needs further elaboration, the visual quality of its buildings, its morphology, together with the ways residents make living—in a word, informality—presents a deviation against the supposedly formal Chinese city.

My interest in the *chengzhongcun* dates back to 2005. To that date, the urban geography (text)books and scholarly publications available to me were rather unhistorical. It was important to re-introduce Western urban geography methods and theories to China. Little attention was given to critical comparisons between the trajectories of urban develop- ment in the West, in China, and in other parts of the world. At that time, scholar interest on the *chengzhongcun* was on the rise. I wondered why and how this kind of community comes into being, and where it is heading to. Does it make any sense to relate it to, say, the urban villages in Boston of the 1950s? Thus, when the opportunity came for me to pursuit a doctorate, I decided to not just study the *chengzhongcun*, but also slums in global urban history.

A WORLD OF SLUMS?

The second half of the twentieth century was the time for global urbanisa- tion. "Whereas in 1900 a mere 10% of the global population were urban dwellers, that percentage now exceeds 50% and will rise even more in the next 50 years. More than 95% of the net increase in the global popula- tion will be in cities of the developing world" (Grimm et al., 2008). Mike Davis compares the overtaking of the 50% threshold of global urbanisa- tion rate to historic epochs such as "Neolithic or Industrial Revolutions" (Davis, 2006). It has to be noted that most of the urbanisation in recent decades took place in countries and regions in the Global South. The city represents employment opportunities, education, medical care, etc. For this reason, it has always been the destination for immigrants pursuing a better life chance. However, cities in the developing world suffer from the gigantic deficits in infrastructure investment, which means a large portion of the new urbanite had to find abode in informal housings, including the slum. From Manila to Lagos, and from Lima to New Delhi, slums mushroomed in and around the city. It is a daily experience of nearly a billion people in the cities of the developing world (UN-Habitat, 2003). The problem of the slum is so rampant that Davis warns that we may be living in "a world of slums".

The fact of living in the city is not in itself a guarantee to a higher living standard. Moreover, without a full citizenship and the rights that it entails, newcomers in the city are essentially the outsiders. The city sets constraints on individual and institutional levels. Employment, for instance, could be a mechanism of entry control at the individual level, i.e. professional qualifications, or at the institutional level in the form of exclusive prerequisite of the "right" type of citizenship. Urban housing, too, is an effective means of exclusion. Besides the dilapidated housing conditions, underneath the visible "surface" of the slum there is the social dynamics that predestined and underpinned its very existence. By calling a place slum, it refers as much to the physical settings as to the social and historical features. To blame the slum for being some sort of "urban ill" will not help to solve the problem except for stigmatizing the place and the people living there (Gilbert, 2007). The first step toward the understanding and the solution of the slum problem is perhaps a revisit of all what we know about the slum, the city, and the framework in which we distinguish the slum from the city.

On the other hand, the ubiquitous presence of slums in developing world cities is deceptive as if it is a peculiar problem for these countries. To be sure, the slum has lost relevance in the daily life in the developed world. It is not to say, of course, there is no problem of urban poverty, marginal ethnic enclaves, etc. However, as a matter of fact, for the most part of the urban history since the Industrial Revolution, the slum was also a integral part of cities in the now "developed" world. Take Britain as an example, slums appeared in many of its cities no later than the early 1820s. It was not until the interwar period that effective slums clearance projects were planned, and the mission was not accomplished until the post-war period (Gilbert, 2019). "The interest of socialist planners in British urban planning stems not only from its widespread application and depth of experience in the United Kingdom but more particularly from the practical welfare approach that it adopted after 1880 to solve problems, identified especially by [Friedrich] Engels, in cities which in Britain were then at the same stage of industrialization that is currently under way in the socialist countries" (French & Hamilton, 1979: 2). The slum, it seems, is deeply rooted in the political economy of the city, and the urban history of the Global North is not irrelevant to the discussion on the slum problem in developing countries.

POST-REFORM URBAN CHINA
STUDIES AND THE *CHENGZHONGCUN*

Urban studies re-emerged in China in the early 1980s. Deng Xiaoping's reform since the late 1970s normalized not only political and economic relations but also academic communications with the West. Four decades later, there are purposefully established international research networks and associations on Urban China studies, including urban planning. Conferences are usually attended by hundreds of people from all over the world, and the working language is English or at least bi-lingual.

What is a Chengzhongcun?

Simply put, the colloquial phrase *chengzhongcun* (城中村. Also known as urban village or village-in-the-city in many English language literature[2]) denotes a former rural village that has been engulfed by the expanding city. In due course, the villagers lose access to their agricultural land for compensations. In some cases, the village collective remain in control of the land on which the houses were built. Typically, the villagers also seek for a replacement of the loss of agricultural income by self-building extra rooms and letting it out. As mentioned before, this kind of encircled, island-like site of settlement is often found along the urban fringe. In more developed regions in China, such as the Pearl River Delta (PRD), many of the *chengzhongcuns* have undergone intensive reconstruction and grown vertically. They certainly do not look like a typical village in the region a few decades ago, and yet they are not yet a part of the city in many senses. Notwithstanding its over-simplicity, many officials and academics would use phrases such as "half-urban, half-rural" (Pinyin: *bancheng banxiang*) to qualitatively describe the *chengzhongcuns*.

The *chengzhongcun* as a hybrid settlement is not defined in legal terms. Nonetheless, it is still possible to draw a profile of the *chengzhongcun*. Rural land in China including that of the *chengzhongcun* is, as stipulated in the *Land Management Law of People's Republic of China*,[3] owned by

---

[2] For comparison on the several translations of this term in English, see: Chung 2010; Liu 2019.

[3] It was preceded by the *Land Reform Law of People's Republic of China*, in effect between June 28, 1950 and November 24, 1987. The latest revision was made on August 26, 2019.

the peasants' collective (with certain exceptional enclaves that are owned, just like the land of the city, by the state). The buildings on the land of the *chengzhongcun* can be either privately owned by the villagers or collectively owned by the community. The construction of buildings in the village is largely spontaneous, although permission from the land management authority should be obtained in advance. The municipal authority of the adjacent city also has the mandate to enforce planning regulations such as height and density on the buildings inside the *chengzhongcun*.

This dual land system is complemented by the *hukou* system. The *hukou* system was launched on January 9 1958, and despite repeated calls of revision is still in effect. In the same logic as the land and the institutions upon the land being categorized as state-owned or collective-owned, the population is also categorized into rural or urban *hukou* holders. In practice, the *hukou* system is intrinsically urban biased. For more than three decades, it largely deterred rural migration to the city because people without an urban *hukou* rural immigrants would have no access to basic livelihood needs or social welfare, including food, housing, employment, medical care, education, etc. in the city.

Chengzhongcun residents can roughly be divided into natives and immigrants. The native residents are supposed to have rural *hukou* since their community is a village. Domestic migrants from rural areas started to pour into the city in the 1980s when the reform lessened the control on the city. Partial market mechanisms were reintroduced as a means to regulate access to livelihood provisions. Rural migrants could stay for long terms in the city. However, it is not just rural migrants who would come to live in the *chengzhongcun*. The non-native residents may come from cities or towns in other municipalities or provinces, and may not be rural *hukou* holders. These are in many cases educated young people trying to reduce housing costs in a destination city. Although rather unusual, native citizens might also move in to live in the *chengzhongcun*.

Chengzhongcun *Emerged as a Research Topic*

Most of the studies on the *chengzhongcun* trace its origin to the Pearl River Delta in Southern China in the mid-1980s. This region, thanks to its proximity to Hong Kong, was the first region to benefit from foreign investment after the reform. Deng Xiaoping's "Southern Tour" [Pinyin: *nanxun*] in 1992 dispelled any remaining ideological confusions, and effectively kicked off a new era of urban development. One of the earliest doctoral dissertations on the *chengzhongcun* has recorded a group of related terms that were in use by the turn of 1990s (Zhang, 2003. His PhD was defended in 1998). *Chengzhongcun* was one of the popular terms, but other terms, such as "dushi cunzhuang" (literally, metropolitan village) or "dushi li de cunzhuang" (literally, village in the metropolis), were also widely used. The later was also used in a somewhat more formal manner, such as in book titles, and *chengzhongcun* was a colloquial abbreviation indicating the same type of community. In retrospective, the coexistence of similar terms could perhaps be better understood as an indicator of the chaos and confusion over the dramatic transformation that Deng was determined to push through. Nonetheless, the term *chengzhongcun* had already reached Northern China no later than 1994 when a journalist published a popular "social documentation" style book in which he apply it in Beijing (Hao, 1994).

From the end of the 1990s onwards, the *chengzhongcun* has become a popular topic within the Chinese language world. The Guangzhou-based Sun Yat-sen University (SYSU) pioneered in the study of *chengzhongcun*. In addition to the above-mentioned Zhang's dissertation (on the theme of generation and transformation dynamics), there were at least three more doctoral studies between 2001–2004.

Kang explored the legal and constitutional framework of *chengzhongcun* redevelopment (Kang, 2005). Sociologists, such as Li Peilin, documented the demise of suburban villages in Guangzhou in the light of "the end of the village" (Li, 2004). Lan meticulously documented the transformation of village communities against the backdrop of economic development and the reshuffling of local government structures (Lan, 2004). Other studies covered a wide spectrum of topics ranging from property right to spatial ordering, and from community governance to urban renewal. However, as China's breakneck urbanisation process slows down in the past few years, it seems that the Chinese academia is about to forsake the *chengzhongcun* as a research topic. Take journal publications as an example, data retrieved from the China National Knowledge Infrastructure (CNKI), a leading national bibliographic service provider, shows that it soared in the first long decade of this century before entering a period of gradual recession (Fig. 1.2).

On the other hand, as early as in the early 1990s, some researchers have hinted that the *chengzhongcun* is the harbinger of profound changes in Chinese history, i.e. the start of the epoch of an urbanised China. Anthropologist Gregory Eliyu Guldin had edited a volume called *Farewell*

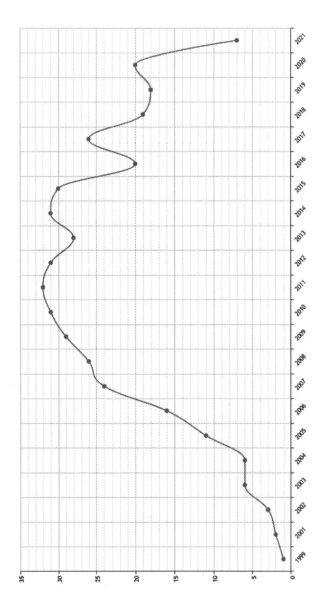

Fig. 1.2 Journal Papers on *chengzhongcun* in Chinese Social Sciences Citation Index (CSSCI) (*Source* https://kns.cnki. net/kns8/defaultresult/index, accessed August 30 2021)

to Peasant China (Guldin, 1997). Zhou Daming, from SYSU, brought this type of neighbourhood (he called it "urban village") into the English language academia on the basis of a paper he had published two years before (Zhou, 1995). The first English journal paper to explicitly include *chengzhongcun* in its title was not published until 2003 (Zhang et al., 2003). Between 2003 and 2021, 55 papers have been published on the topic of *chengzhongcun* in journals included in the Web of Science Core Collection. 2018 tops the annual spread with 12 papers published in that year. Besides, there were also publications in languages other than English (see for instance in German, Herrle et al., 2008).

The *chengzhongcun* was also an inspiration to architects to reflect on Chinese urbanism. One of the most successful story was the *chengzhongcun* redevelopment projects by Meng Yan's team in Shenzhen (URBANUS, 2006). In 2008, the journal *Architectural Design* published a guest-edited special issue on "New Urban China". The Rotterdam based architect Yushi Uehara developed a powerful visual representation of the life circle of the *chengzhongcun* (Uehara, 2008. He used *village in the city* [ViC]). In her work on Chinese urban property development, Hsing showcased the way how the village collective transformed itself into some kind of corporation to take advantage of its ownership of the land that eventually lead to the advanced form of *village in the city* (Hsing, 2010). The *chengzhongcun's* potential as an urban incubator for rural immigrants is documented through an ethnographic study in Shenzhen (Bach, 2010).

THE *CHENGZHONGCUN* QUESTION AT LARGE

At the beginning of this century, in an effort to coordinate the global campaign against urban poverty, the United Nations set up the Millennium Development Goals (MDGs). One of its targets was to make "a significant improvement in the lives of at least 100 million slum dwellers by 2020" (Fig. 1.3). However, even though the MDGs was pronounced a success (United Nations, 2015a), studies show that slum is still an acute problem in many parts of the world (Shibata et al., 2015; Sengupta & Benjamin, 2016; Soederberg, 2017). When it comes to international coordination, foreign development aids tend to be directed onto projects concerning fundamental livelihoods, such as agriculture modernisation or infrastructure construction, rather than uplifting of basic living standards in places such as the slum. While in many cases the slum is indeed a place

Fig. 1.3 A Billboard with Summary of the Millennium Development Goals (MDGs) in India (*Source* Photo taken by the author on February 27 2009, Kolkata, India)

in dire need of improvement, it enjoys no priority compared to other issues equally if not more urgent and demanding. Other civil agencies, such as NGOs, have been active on the field for decades. The problem of the slum, it seems, is after all a local problem and the responsibilities to redevelop often rest in the hands of those who are neither local nor foreign to it.

The Sustainable Development Goals (SDGs) aim to "ensure access for all to adequate, safe and affordable housing and basic services and upgrade slums" (United Nations, 2015b). Important as it is, the slum problem is not just about insecure water supply or precarious housing or lack of toilets. It is as social and political as it is physical. "[i]t is clear that, without solving the problem of unemployment and poorly paid work, any promise to solve the problem of slums and shantytowns is bound to fail" (Gilbert, 2019: 8). If we understand the slum as the space of containment, from the point of view of the ruling urban regime, then can it be a space of resistance or revolt? Will it also become a new front of civil struggle for social justice? The slum has the potential to challenge the legitimacy and long term sustainability of a given social structure. In this sense, it is also imperative to compare the experiences of slum struggles across the globe.

In the end of 2020, the Chinese government officially announced its victory in the fight against absolute poverty. President Xi Jinping remarked that "China has lifted all rural poor population under the current standard out of poverty and nearly 100 million poor people have shaken off poverty" (Xie & Zhang, 2020). Elsewhere, the timeline of this anti-poverty campaign is outlined (Xinhua News Agency, 2021), and it is highlighted that China was the first developing country to have met the MDGs target of poverty reduction in 2015. It was achieved largely through immense domestic transfer payment to its western provinces and rural areas. Infrastructure and industry are the most preferred fields of investment. This campaign also aims to enhance poorer region's competitiveness and sustainability by introducing tailored programs in agriculture, industry, service, or tourism, etc. Generally speaking, regarding poverty alleviation, the Chinese government's attention is set on rural revitalization rather than *chengzhongcun* redevelopment, which is primarily the concern of the municipal governments.

Already in the early 2010s, there was a sense of optimism among urban China specialists and urban planning officials who hold that the *chengzhongcun* was about to become a thing of the past. It was well studied, documented, and above all comprehended. In a way, this optimism is not without a reason. Zhu Rongji's urban housing reform in the late 1990s paved the way to a urban housing market in China. This reform favours those who had already at the advantageous position at the cost the general populace (Logan et al., 2010). The financialisation of the urban housing market further strengthens its nature as asset over that of shelter and results in soaring property prices. One of the direct effects is that native villagers of the *chengzhongcuns* welcome the redevelopment on their community even if that means demolishing and relocation (Fig. 1.4). Compensation, either in the form of new housing or in cash payment, is offered to villagers. Immigrants and other non-native residents of the *chengzhongcuns* are excluded, on the basis of their *hukou*, from the negotiation process. Strong urban entrepreneurialism—competitive compensation packages to pacify native villagers, or in another expression, to "share the fruits of urban development" (Pinyin: *gongxiang chengshi fazhan chengguo*)—in a weak civil society means that the *chengzhongcun* is undefended against the urban regime.

Fig. 1.4 *Chengzhongcun* Demolished to Make Room for Urban Redevelopment (*Source* Photo taken by the author on June 30 2010, Shanghai, China)

It is hardly surprising that most of the studies on the *chengzhongcun* repeatedly analyze it within technical frameworks of land ownership, spatial configuration, institutional exclusion, etc. There is an uneasy absence of historical-cultural and comparative perspectives. As such, these analyses seldom include in-depth discussion on the long term rural–urban relationship and interaction. Equally noticeable is that, while many scholars have rightfully pointed out that the *chengzhongcun* phenomenon is unique to China, very few have tried to relate it with similar communities, such as the slum or *favela*, in other developing countries. For general readers who are not familiar China, it takes extra efforts to put the jigsaw together to form a full picture of the "Global Slum".

Structure of the Book

This book is based on my doctoral dissertation at KU Leuven, Belgium (January 2012). To prepare it, I spent a considerable part of my doctoral student years in the field. Whenever I travelled back to China, I would visit some of the *chengzhongcuns*. In 2009, I had the opportunity to visit India and Brazil, both trips helped me to gain first hand experience of the Indian slum and Brazilian *favela*. On the other hand, during study trips, I visited a number of cities and towns in Belgium, France, and Germany together KU Leuven faculties and students. The itineraries included some of the disadvantaged areas in and around the European cities. I also travelled around on my own into some ethnic enclaves. They were vital for me to formulate a framework in which the developing world cities could be better positioned and understood.

In a way, it feels like preparing a second version of a published book (but it is not!) when I begin making updates and revisions to the original dissertation. I feel strong sympathy to Herbert J. Gans' words he put in the preface of a 1982 edition of his work, "*The Levittowners* is now fifteen years old, and some of its observations are not applicable at the moment" (Gans, 1982: xi). The post-PhD decade has given me a privilege to first distance myself from this topic and then come back with a refreshed sensibility. I have worked in an urban planning department before taking up the current post as a historical geographer, and occasionally I still work with urban planners and other urbanists. The text to follow, of course, contains both the originals and updates made to reflect the current stage of affairs.

The main text is organized into five chapters. Chapter Two is a reflection on the historical geography of the city as an ideal. As per its namesake, the *chengzhongcun* conveys an image of contrast between the city and its other, i.e. the village. Therefore, it is imperative to examine the rural–urban relationship from a historical perspective and trace its root in the urban historical geography tradition. I will briefly outline the process through which the city gained its superior position against the countryside by constituting citizenship as a mechanism to distinguish. To that end, I will refer to the generation(s) of European urbanists active at the turn and early decades of the twentieth century.

Chapter Three is on the political economy of the *chengzhongcun*. While the *chengzhongcun* is often conceived as a recent Chinese phenomenon of urban informal housing, I challenge this view in two ways. By debunking the intrinsic dilemma of the right to (urban) housing, I reconnect the current Chinese urban housing issue to its predecessor, i.e. the Soviet system, which is downplayed or even forgotten in China nowadays. How does China deal with its Soviet legacy? I argue that, in fact, it is still a force in the making of Chinese cities. On the other hand, some further clarifications are needed to better understand the *chengzhongcun*. The *chengzhongcun* should not be confused with the more recent urban village movement in Britain. The slightly distant American urban village phenomenon, as examined by Herbert J. Gans, would be a more appropriate reference in urban history.

Chapter Four is based on my fieldwork and survey in two *chengzhongcuns* in Shanghai and Hefei in 2009. Existing empirical studies on the *chengzhongcun* are in abundance. Yet, so far, little attention has been directed towards *chengzhongcun* residents' *perceptions*. How the people who actually live there think of their community, especially at a time when demolishing and relocation is the conventional approach of urban renewal and redevelopment? What are the most difficult obstacles toward urban integration? This study is one of the first to probe if there is any relationship between *chengzhongcun* residents' social-economic profiles and their views.

If the *chengzhongcun* is taken as the Chinese counterpart of the slum or *favela*, can it also become a space of resistance? In Chapter Five I explore the possibility of using public art in the struggle for citizenship rights in the *chengzhongcun*. In most cases, the majority of *chengzhongcun* residents are rural *hukou* holders. Among them, the rural immigrant suffer the most from the *hukou* system. Their civil rights, such as the right to education for their children, are severely restricted in the city. In a case study of Hefei, members of the civil society intervened and used public art as a means to articulate on immigrants' behalf. It is a rare event in many senses, but it showcases a mode of interaction between the urban middle class and the deprived immigrants.

The Sixth Chapter relates the emerging slum tourism phenomenon found in several developing countries with its closest counterparts in China. Slum tourism is hailed as an effective means of community development, albeit at the meantime also gets a lot of criticism on ethics front such as poverty voyeurism. Through two case studies taking place in and around the *chengzhongcun* in southern China, I argue that slum tourism could be a effective approach towards more inclusive urban development.

In the Conclusion, I re-embed this work into the general question of urbanism in China. If, as Frederick W. Mote points out, it is the rural elements that define Chinese way of life, what kind of consequences will China's current urbansation process produce? It has to noted that by no means do I intend to dwell upon the exceptionality of the *chengzhongcun*. Quite on the contrary, I come back to the similarities and differences between the *chengzhongcun*, the slum, and the different types of urban village. It is hope that a brief study like this one on the urban–rural interface at a time when China is about the tipping point of urbanisation would shed some light on the quality and fate of the Chinese civilisation.

References

Bach, J. (2010). "They come in peasants and leave citizens": Urban villages and the making of Shenzhen, China. *Cultural Anthropology, 25*(3), 421–458. https://doi.org/10.1111/j.1548-1360.2010.01066.x

Chung, H. (2010). Building an image of villages-in-the-city: A clarification of China's distinct Urban spaces. *International Journal of Urban and Regional Research, 34*(2), 421–437. https://doi.org/10.1111/j.1468-2427.2010.009 79.x

Davis, M. (2006). *Planet of the slums*. Verso.

Douglass, M., Wissink, B., & van Kempen, B. (2012). Enclave urbanism in China: Consequences and interpretations. *Urban Geography, 33*(2), 167–182. https://doi.org/10.2747/0272-3638.33.2.167

French, R. A., & Hamilton, F. E. I. (1979). Is there a socialist city? In R. A. French, & F. E. I. Hamilton (Eds.), *The socialist city: Spatial structure and urban policy*. John Wiley & Sons.

Gans, H. J. (1962). *The urban villagers: Group and class in the life of Italian-American*. The Free Press.

Gans, H. J. (1967). *The Levittowners: Ways of life and politics in a new suburban community*. Pantheon Books.

Gans, H. J. (1982). *The Levittowners: Ways of life and politics in a new suburban community*. Columbia University Press.

Gans, H. J. (2007). Remembering the urban villagers and its location in intellectual time: A response to zukin. *City & Community, 6*(3), 231–236. https://doi.org/10.1111/j.1540-6040.2007.00215_1.x

Gilbert, A. (2007). The return of the slum: Does language matter? *International Journal of Urban and Regional Research, 31*(4), 697–713. https://doi.org/10.1111/j.1468-2427.2007.00754.x

Gilbert, A. (2019). Slums and Shanties. In Anthony M. Orum (Ed.), *The Wiley Blackwell Encyclopedia of urban and regional studies*. Wiley-Blackwell, pp. 1–9. https://doi.org/10.1002/9781118568446.eurs0286

Grimm, N. B., Faeth, S. H., Golubiewski, N. E., Redman, C. L., Wu, J., Bai, X., & Briggs, J. M. (2008). Global change and the ecology of cities. *Science, 319*, 756–760. https://doi.org/10.1126/science.1150195

Guldin, G. E. (1997). *Farewell to Peasant China: Rural urbanization and social change in the late twentieth century*. M.E. Sharpe.

Hao, Z. (1994). *Adventuring the world recklessly* [Pinyin: wangming chuang tianxia]. Cultural Union Press of China.

He, S. J., & Wu, F. L. (2009). China's emerging neoliberal urbanism: Perspectives from urban redevelopment. *Antipode, 41*(2), 282–304. https://doi.org/10.1111/j.1467-8330.2009.00673.x

Herrle, P., Ipsen, D., Nebel, S., & Weichler, H. (2008). Wie Bauern die mega-urbane Landschaft in Suedchina Praegen: Zur Rolle der "Urban Villages" bei der Entwicklung der Perlflussdeltas. *Geographische Rundschau, 60*(11), 38–46.

Hsing, Y. T. (2010). *The great urban transformation: Politics of land and property in China*. Oxford University Press.

Iossifova, D. (2015). Borderland urbanism: Seeing between enclaves. *Urban Geography, 36*(1), 90–108. https://doi.org/10.1080/02723638.2014.961365

Kang, B. (2005). *Urban housing demolishment and relocation, and the application of law in Chengzhongcun redevelopment* [Pinyin: chengshi fangwu chaiqian ji chengzhongcun gaizao de falv shiyong]. People's Court Publishing House.

Lan, Y. Y. (2004). *Villages in the metropolis: Field studies on a new village community* [Pinyin: dushi li de cunzhuang: yige xin cunshe gongtongti de shidi yanjiu]. SDX Joint Publishing Company.

Li, P. (2004). *The end of the village: Stories from Yangcheng village* [Pinyin: cunluo de zhongjie: yangchengcun de gushi]. Commercial Press.

Liu, Y. T. (2019) Village in the city. *The Wiley Blackwell Encyclopedia of urban and regional studies*. Wiley Blackwell. https://doi.org/10.1002/978111856 8446.eurs0408

Logan, J. R., Fang, Y. P., & Zhang, Z. X. (2010). The winners in China's urban housing reform. *Housing Studies, 25*(1), 101–117. https://doi.org/10.1080/02673030903240660

Ning, J. Z. (2021). *Key data of the Seventh Census of China* [diqici quanguo renkoupucha zhuyao shuju qingkuang]. National Bureau of Statistics, http://www.stats.gov.cn/tjsj/zxfb/202105/t20210510_1817176.html [accessed Aug. 11 2021].

Oakes, T. (2019). Happy town: Cultural governance and biopolitical urbanism in China. *Environment and Planning A—Economy and Space, 51*(1), 244–262. https://doi.org/10.1177/0308518X17693621

Pooley C., & Lawton R. (1988). The social geography of nineteenth century British cities: A review. In D. Denecke, & G. Shaw (Ed.), *Urban Historical Geography: Recent Progress in Britian and Germany*. Cambridge University Press.

Sengupta, P., & Benjamin, A. I. (2016). Countdown 2015: An assessment of basic provision to migrant families in the urban slums of Ludhiana, North India. *Environment & Urbanization, 28*(2), 569–582.https://doi.org/10.1177/0956247816647339

Shanghai Academy of Social Sciences. (1962). *The transformation of Shanty Towns in Shanghai* [Pinyin: Shanghai Penghuqu de Bianqian]. Shanghai People's Press.

Shibata, T., Wilson, J. L., Watson, L. M., Nikitin, I. V., Ansariadi, Ane, R. L., & Maidin, A. (2015). Life in a landfill slum, children's health, and the Millennium Development Goals. *Science of the Total Environment, 536*, 408–418.https://doi.org/10.1016/j.scitotenv.2015.05.137

Soederberg, S. (2017). Universal access to affordable housing? Interrogating an Elusive Development Goal. *Globalizations, 14*(3), 343–359.https://doi.org/10.1080/14747731.2016.1253937

Uehara, Y. (2008). Unknown urbanity: Towards the village in the city. In L. Liauw (Ed.), "New Urban China", a special issue of the *Architectural Design*, 78(5), 52–55. https://doi.org/10.1002/ad.738

UN-Habitat. (2003). *Slums of the world: The face of urban poverty in the new millennium?* https://unhabitat.org/slums-of-the-world-the-face-of-urban-poverty-in-the-new-millennium [accessed September 9 2011].

United Nations. (2015a). *The Millennium Development Goals Report 2015*. https://www.un.org/millenniumgoals/2015_MDG_Report/pdf/MDG%202015%20rev%20(July%201).pdf [accessed May 30 2021].

United Nations. (2015b). *Transforming Our World: The 2030 Agenda for Sustainable Development*. https://sdgs.un.org/2030agenda [accessed May 30 2021].

URBANUS. (2006). *VILLAGE/CITY; CITY/VILLAGE* [cun/cheng; cheng/cun]. China Electric Power Press. [in Chinese].

Whyte, W. F. (1943). *Street corner society: The social structure of an Italian slum*. University of Chicago Press.

Wong, T. C., & Liu, R. (2017). Developmental urbanism, city image branding and the "Right to the city" in transitional China. *Urban Policy and Research*, *35*(2), 210–223. https://doi.org/10.1080/08111146.2015.1122587

Woodworth, M. D. (2018). Landscape and the cultural politics of China's anticipatory urbanism. *Landscape Research*, *43*(7), 891–905. https://doi.org/10.1080/01426397.2017.1404020

Wu, F. L. (2010). *China's emerging cities: The making of new urbanism*. Routledge.

Wu, F. L., Zhang, F. Z., & Webster, C. (Eds.). (2014). *Rural migrants in urban China: Enclaves and transient urbanism*. Routledge.

Xie, J., & Zhang, Y. Y. (2020). *Xi announces major victory in poverty alleviation*. Xinhua News Agency, http://www.xinhuanet.com/english/2020-12/04/c_139561843.htm [accessed May 14 2021].

Xinhua News Agency. (2021). *Timeline: China's fight against poverty*. http://en.qstheory.cn/2021-02/25/c_596070.htm [accessed May 14 2021].

Zhang, J. (2003). *A study on the chengzhongcuns of Guangzhou* [Pinyin: Guangzhou chengzhongcun yanjiu]. Guangzhou: People's Publishing Housing of Guangdong.

Zhou, D. M. (1995). On rural urbanization in China. *Chinese Sociology & Anthropology* (renamed as *Chinese Sociological Review* since 2011), *28*(2), 9–46. https://doi.org/10.2753/CSA0009-462528029

CHAPTER 2

The City and Its Other: A Brief Historical Geography

Abstract This chapter offers a brief historical–geographical review on the genesis of urbanism. Drawing on the literature of urban history and sociology, notably that of Henri Pirenne and Max Weber, the rise of the city is approached from the perspective of the institutionalization of the urban against the rural. The outcasts in Chinese cities from the imperial times to the Repulican period are introduced through literature review. In light of that, it is stressed that the contemporary *chengzhongcun* issue should be comprehended with a more informed awareness of its broader relevance. Importantly, the several radically different ways in which the term "urban village" has been adopted are highlighted. An oxymoron in its own right, the nostalgia of a past or lost ideal of British village life should not be confused with its contemporary connotations in the Chinese context.

Keywords Urbanism · Henri Pirenne · Urban village · Urban outcast · "Random conceptual appropriation"

> *It is our belief that the concentration of wealth in the hands of certain social groups or classes was indeed – and this does not make us Marxist! – a fundamental factor in the historical development [of the city].* (Verhulst, 1999: 153)

Oxymorons are terms that are etymologically paradoxical, and "urban village" is a good example. If a village is urban enough, then is it still justified to be called a village? Questions like this would pop up along the way as we approach the core of the urban–rural relationship. It is difficult to draw a clear line between what is urban and what is rural, and yet the urban–rural relationship is often rendered as a dichotomy, which deeply affects the people's lives in the process of urbanisation. In order to dispel this mysticism about the city and urbanity, I will take a historical–geographical perspective on the rise of the city as an antagonistic power against the countryside. Specifically, I examine the institutionalisation of urban superiority via the establishment of citizenship. In the meantime, I also compare the urban theories that are derived from European and American experiences with that from Chinese urban developments. In so doing, it will put Chinese urbanity, historical and contemporary, into perspective.

The Great Urban Awakening in Europe

Origin of the City

Engin Isin was right to point out that "the question of the origins of cities will continue to fascinate historians and urbanists" (Isin, 2002: 6). We are living in an urban world and there is no doubt about that. So profoundly urban that it is almost difficult to think of the world as a predominantly rural planet just about one century ago. Take Britain as an example, in 1801 the urban population in England and Wales represents only one third of their population. However, by the middle of nineteenth century, the ratio has reached a threshold of 50% (Morris & Rodger, 1993: 2). Thanks to the Industrial Revolution, mass urbanization was made possible in the nineteenth century. The impulse of making sense of urban living has been shared by both intellectuals and revolutionaries.

Seen from a distance in time, the late nineteenth and early twentieth century have produced some of the founding fathers of urban studies. Sociology, for instance, reflected the curiosity and perhaps also wariness over the diverse modes in which social groups lived and worked together in compacted spaces. George Simmel, for instance, studied the mental life of the people living in the city in his 1903 seminal work, *The Metropolis and Mental Life*. Simmel's influence on Louis Wirth, the author of the all-time classic 1938 essay *Urbanism as a Way of Life*, is obvious. The city environment is artificial, and it exerts profound impacts on the human mind. Robert Park, also "used geography as a means of defining human ecology" (Entrikin, 1980).

Late nineteenth century scholars were not only interested in the new urban society, but also in the history of the rise of the city.[1] It matters because the other side of the coin is the retreat of the countryside. To understand the rural–urban relationship, it is necessary to understand first how the city acquired the superior status *vis-à-vis* the villages. To probe the spatiality of the city and load the urbanity onto the temporal axis, it unavoidably involves some sort of structuralist framework. It aims to answer questions such as where was the city, when did it emerge, and more importantly, why is it a city. Hardly surprising, "modern urban geographer looks at the origins of cities as one of a number of social scientists concerned with a common problem" (Carter, 1983: 1). It is worth noting that the interest in the origins of the city was by and large a "Continental" topic.[2] German scholars were the first group in Europe to develop an interest in the history and social organizations of the city in the nineteenth century. Perhaps due to their extraordinary history with free cities stand next to feudal states, and the sweeping nationalism, German scholars had a strong sensibility regarding the unique role of the city. French intellectuals, on the other hand, were equally enthusiastic about the understanding of the city. To them, the city defines Europe. Lucien Febvre once famously made a portrayal of Europe as below:

> The true Europe was the Europe of cities in the middle of the countryside, the Europe that finally came into being from the twelfth century [...] a Europe covered with a tapestry of cities, real cities, cities that were not just fortress, not just granaries and centres of rural administration. (Febvre, 1999: 155, cited in Le Galès, 2002: 34)

Certainly it is an interesting albeit idealized angle on urban and regional development in Europe. In reality, however, the remnants of social segregation are still visible in European cities (Fig. 2.1). The study

---

[1] Henri Pirenne included in his book a selective list of references of the studies on urban origins. See Pirenne (1936: 40).

[2] For a summary of German literature on urban origins since the WWII, see Denecke and Shaw (1988: 24–36).

Fig. 2.1 Portuguese informal settlement ilhas (island or quarter) in Porto (*Source* Photo taken by the author on November 12, 2009, Porto, Portugal)

on the origins of the city could help to provide a structural, albeit tentative, reference to the urban issues of later eras including the contemporary time. By the late twentieth century, it is said that the time is ripe for a critical look "at the concept of an urban revolution and to consider the city as emergent from a longer period of social and economic change and cultural adaptation in which an elaborate complex of factors was mingled" (Carter, 1983: 9). Rather than tracing the emergence of the city into a certain place and moment, a degree of fuzziness must be tolerated here. Nonetheless, some key figures in the study of the city and urbanity, such as the Belgian medieval historian Henri Pirenne, could not simply be overlooked.

Henri Pirenne

Nowadays, even in Belgium, Henri Pirenne (1868–1935) has been reduced to an average medieval historian.[3] No longer does the Belgian nation see him as a national hero, and in the academic world his theory is not popular any more. However, as the founder of the Gent Historical School, his works have inspired not only historians but possibly also researches on general urban issues.

Henri Pirenne was born in Verviers in southeast Belgium. He was a diligent scholar and he authored "some thirty books and three hundred or so articles, notes, reviews and commentaries" (Brundage, 1979). Before taking up his position as a professor of history at Ghent University, he had acquainted both German and French historians in his early study and travelling years (see: Froeyman, 2004; Lyon, 1974). During the year 1884–1885, he went for a study trip to Germany and met some of the most influential figures of the epoch including Gustav Schmoller, Karl Lamprecht, Georg von Below, Siegfried Rietschel and Otto von Gierke. Among other important matters, it is said that Pirenne learnt from Schmoller about the importance of medieval cities (Froeyman, 2004). Writing for a new English translation of Pirenne's *Medieval Cities: Their Origins and the Revival of Trade*, Frank D. Halsey, the English translator, noted that:

> *Medieval Cities* is possibly of even more value today [1969] than when first published [in English in 1925]. In its clear account of the part played by the middle class in the development of the modern economic system and modern culture, it makes us realize how much cities of the present have borrowed and are borrowing from medieval municipal institutions. (Halsey, in Pirenne, 1969: XII)

Bearing both German and French influences, Pirenne was one of the first scholars to study the role cities have played in the formation of the European civilization. In Chapter Six of his *Les Villes du Moyen Age*, Pirenne outlines the process that the citizen class took shape in the cities of Northern Italy and The Netherlands in late medieval times. Importantly, Pirenne puts special attention to the extension of the city, i.e. the building of the new suburb next to the old walled city. He refers to terms

[3] Important updates: the Henri Pirenne Institute for Medieval Studies was founded in Ghent University in 2013.

such as 'burgher' or 'poorter' as the evidence of the connection between the concepts of merchants and urban residents. On another occasion, He made a vivid and nuanced account of the genesis of a city being born out of the Dark Ages: "The wandering life of the merchants […] caused them from the very beginning to seek the protection of the walled towns and burgs, which stood at intervals along the rivers or natural routes by which they travelled" (Pirenne, 1936: 42). This description, however, should read as a metaphor rather than an authentic record of some real city. The city wall is not only a part of the defensive constructions protecting the citizens from outside, but also a symbol of juridical system demarcating the people into insider and outsider. To him, this is the birth of the city: "[I]t is strictly true to say that the medieval town, and consequently the modern town, had its birth in the *faubourg* of the city, or of the *bourg* which determined its site" (Pirenne, 1936: 43).

For medieval cities, the law applied to the insiders does not apply equally to the outsiders. It has taken centuries of struggles to have the concept of "citizen" enlarged so as to include the people of the state as defined by nationality. The word 'citizen' was used to refer to the registered civil status of the people in spite of the actual place of residence, thus goes beyond its exclusivity of city dwellers. This transition is of great importance because this new meaning signaled the shift from the agriculture dominated society towards one that is driven by commerce, industry, and later service. Pirenne had the insight to discern the close resemblance between municipal politics and that of the nation state:

> In general, urban politics were determined by the same sacred egoism which was later to inspire State politics. For the burgess the country population existed only to be exploited. Far from allowing it to enjoy their franchises, they always obstinately refused it all share in them. Nothing could be further removed from the spirit of modern democracy than the exclusiveness with which the medieval towns continued to defend their privileges. (Pirenne, 1936: 57)

This observation is as valid as ever.[4] He claimed that due to the rise of the citizen class, which mostly consists of merchants and immigrants, the

---

[4] Perhaps unsurprisingly that Arrighi, an economic historian and philosopher at the Ferdinand Braudel Centre, put the Dutch United Provinces as the transitory stage from the power of the city to the power of the nation state. See Arrighi (2007: 238).

significance of the city wall as a physical demarcation of social status has diminished although as defence work it continued to exist for another few centuries. Instead, it was the legal system that defined an urban society.

The influence of German methodologies, e.g. the use of a broad range of materials for research, as introduced by German historians including his mentor and friend Karl Lamprecht, is everywhere in his analysis of the fall and revival of cities. It is imperative to compare Pirenne with his great German peer Max Weber (1864–1920). They belong to the same generation of scholars on the city. Despite the absence of direct communications between them, their intellectual similarity could be best observed in the following quotes:

> Freedom became the legal status of the bourgeoisie, so much so that it was no longer a personal privilege only, but a territorial one, inherent in urban soil just as serfdom was in manorial soil. (Pirenne, 1936: 52. Originally published in French in 1933)
>
> The associational character of the city [in Asia] and the concept of a burgher (as contrast to the man from countryside) never developed at all or existed only in rudiments. (Weber, 1968: 1227. Originally published in German in 1922)

It is clear that both of them would agree on the point that it is the association between certain places, e.g. the city, and the legal/social system that defines the city and the West. However, they were, after all, undertaking different disciplines. While Weber was obsessed with the social and institutional infrastructures that lead to the modern capitalism, Pirenne was very attentive to the physical settings in which it took place. This is not to say that Pirenne missed out on the importance of social and institutional forces. Quite on the contrary, he saw the interpretation of the legal system not as an abstract process, but a dynamic and grounded struggle:

> The medieval burgess…was a different kind of person from all who lived outside the town walls. Once outside the gates and the moat we are in another world, or more exactly, in the domain of another law. The acquisition of citizenship brought with it…a peculiar status [,]…which was later to be known as the 'third estate'. (Pirenne, 1936: 56–57)

Nowadays, scholars of geography or sociology are familiar with theories on social-spatial interaction. Back to the early twentieth century, Pirenne was one of the earliest to shed light on physical settings of historical events. This view is explicitly expressed in his *Mohammed and Charle-magne*, in which the rise of Western European cities is attributed, at least partly, to the closure of trade routes to the East. As a matter of fact, there is nothing special to be interested in the Islamic world in the nine-teenth century. However, to interpret historical events within the grand geographical scale like Pirenne did was certainly exceptional.

The Pirenne's Thesis is not without critiques. For instance, his nation-alistic stance in domestic affairs not only helped him to win the fame in the years following WWI, but also caused a lot of suspicions on his academic ethics. "Despite his professional scrupulosity, Pirenne's view on the history of the Low Countries was strongly colored [*sic*] by his fervent nationalism and by his emotional commitment to the essential unity of Walloons and Flemings" (Brundage, 1979). In the realm of research, too, his neglect, if not ignorance, of the Carolingian new cities and antic Italian cities is a loophole in his theory (Froeyman, 2004). His "split" from the German tradition, as a result of his experience during the war, is also problematic because even though he is said to have turned more to the individual figures in history, this reorientation is basically fruitless.

That being said, his contribution to medieval urban history and the history of Belgium has inspired many contemporaries and those after his time. He maintained close contacts with Marc Bloch and Lucien Febvre, the two eminent historians who co-founded the Annales School. On the other hand, his work such as *Mohammed and Charlemagne* certainly set up an example of handling historical events at a grand scale and yet remain nuanced in details that the fellow Annales School historians aspired to. Ferdinand Braudel opened his magnum opus, *The Mediterranean and the Mediterranean World in the Age of Philip II*, with a tribute to Pirenne. Interestingly, Pirenne might have also inspired the famous urbanist Jane Jacobs during her short period of study at the Columbia University back in the 1930s. Ironically, Jane Jacobs in fact opposes Pirenne by arguing that it was not the culmination of commerce that gave birth to the city, but rather the capacity to reorganize trade and agriculture as the replacement of import (see: Jacobs, in Carter, 1983: 5; and Jacobs, 1984).

Although Pirenne's studies belong to the generation before WWII, his thesis remains one of the enduring seminal works in urban history. The reason is because he dealt with the fundamental question of the genesis of the city—not just the moats and walls as can be found in archaeolog-ical sites and traced back to millenniums back into the deep history—but rather the idea of the city that despite the wars and revolutions survived to this day. Its incarnations have been spread to almost every corner on this planet.

CHINESE CITIES AND ITS OUTCASTS

Chinese Exceptionalism?

The Chinese city was a source of fascination for European merchants for hundreds of years (how could we forget Marco Polo?). However, when the contacts became more regular in the nineteenth century, the view on China and Chinese cities could not escape from being affected by "Orientalism". Here I use the double quote mark because historically Orientalism was not intended for China or East Asia, but Sinology was simply not robust enough to question Euro-centralism in the Humanities and Social Sciences. Writing about the resurgence of African urban studies in the 2000s, Myers has criticized the "African Exceptionalism" for missing out the point that instead of pinpointing the limits of theoretical applicability, it resorts to the emphasis of uniqueness (Myers, 2011: 101). There is the effort to counter balance the exceptionalism of one kind or another in urban studies notably championed by the geographer Jennifer Robinson.

In the past few decades geographers, planners and architects have made a lot of efforts to emancipate urban studies and to support its growth from rudimentary status to a popular topic. Among the heatedly debated issues is the Weber thesis. In his master piece *Economy and Society*, Weber dedicated a chapter to the categorization of cities. In Section Eight of this chapter, he said that "the Asian cities did not know a special substantive or trial law applicable to the 'burghers' by virtue of their membership in the city-commune, or a court autonomously appointed by them" (Weber, 1968: 1227). Specifically, he wrote on China:

> This [Chinese cities' lack of autonomy] can be explained in terms of the different origins of the occidental and oriental city. The polis of Antiquity originated as an overseas trading city, however strong its base in land-lordism, but China was predominantly an inland area...[and] the prosperity of the Chinese city did not primarily depend upon the citizens' enterprising spirit in economic and political ventures but rather upon the imperial administration, especially the administration of the rivers. (Weber, 1951: 15–16)

Unlike Pirenne whose interests of research are mostly focused on Europe, Weber spared no effort in formatting a general scheme in which the East and the West were treated separately. As a matter of fact, the Eurocentric perspective did not originate from him. Karl Marx had coined the term "Asiatic Mode of Production". It seems that the nineteenth century scholars, perhaps influenced by colonialism, were eager to take up a relative perspective using Europe as a point of reference in the same way like the prime meridian. To Marx, the self-sufficient and remotely connected villages are the origin of "rural idiocy". Max Weber's judgement that river management would result in the lack of free cities was inherited by Karl Wittfogel (1957). Wittfogel was known for the thesis on the hydraulic society and despotic governance. It was a new incarnation of geographical determinism, as a form of dialectics of nature, emerged ever since the Enlightenment Movement.

The City in Late Imperial China is a collection of papers that put forward for the first time a comprehensive examination on historical development of Chinese cities on topics including the urban network, planning thoughts, morphology, and urban economics, etc. (Skinner, 1977). Importantly, because it was published right before China's reform, it has influenced more than a generation of Chinese scholars. A key argument, among others, in that book is that urban development in China was significantly different from that in Europe. In specific, historically Chinese cities still preserved so much links with the countryside that independent urban communities were never to be formed at a noteworthy scale. To give an example, it is believed that "the idea that the city represents either a distinct style or, more important, a higher level of civilization than the countryside is a cliché of our Western cultural traditions" (Mote, 1977: 102). Mote was studying the city of Nanjing and he concluded that in pre-modern Chinese cities do not possess an essentially different quality than the countryside. If we were to agree with his view, then we must also answer the question of when and how the Chinese cities acquired the otherwise non-indigenous character of urban superiority.

That observation was, however, not far from the Weberian view. Interestingly, since the 1980s, there was a counter movement in Sinology, namely the "Seeing China from a Chinese Perspective". It was aimed to adjust the Eurocentric view of Sinologists who are mostly European and North American. The outcomes include, among other works, William L. Rowe's study on the urban society of modern Hankow (Rowe, 1984). Rowe believed that, contrary to the popular belief that Chinese cities in the pre-modern era were lacking urban features, the port city of Hankow (Hankou, now part of the city of Wuhan) had more commonalities with European cities than differences. Kenneth Pomeranz goes even further to challenge the creed that it was liberalism and/or market that lead to the divergence between the fate of China and West Europe before the nineteenth century (Pomeranz, 2001). Specifically, he argues that the expansion of the European colonies facilitated the rise of Europe, which otherwise could have been as static as East Asia. The role of the city in this great divergence is remarkable.

Outcasts in Chinese Cities, Then and Now

But, if the city in pre-modern China is not the place to differentiate people, why are there outcasts in its vicinity? In the late eighteenth century, the Qing (1664–1911) court imposed strict controls upon overseas trades and designated Canton (Guangzhou) as the only regular trading port. was designated as the only trading port. Thanks to the intercontinental trade, legends of the city could reach as far as Scotland to allow Adam Smith to refer to Canton as an example of how human labour could be misplaced:

> In the neighborhood of Canton many hundred, it is commonly said, many thousand families have no habitation on the land, but live constantly in little fishing boats upon the rivers and the canals. (Smith, 2007: 47–48. Originally published in 1776)

He continued to point out the miserable living conditions of this population is worse than any underclass of European cities. Unfortunately, it is difficult to verify the source, which is certainly interesting, from which Smith drew this reference. But the credibility, rather than precision, of this story is beyond doubt. Chinese gentry and officials had noticed this peculiar group in the cities of the Pearl River Delta in their reports long before and after Smith's time. In the case of Guangzhou, these people are very likely to be the Tankas (Pinyin: *danmin*).

The Tanka people are known as the "boat people" due to their distinct tradition of living in the boat, instead of on land, along the rivers in several South-eastern provinces of China. In large cities such as Fuzhou, Guangzhou, and later in Hong Kong, they conglomerate to form an outcast community. Nowadays, they are thought of constituting an ethnic group, although little is known about the social and cultural associations between the numerous Tanka communities across southern China. Historians and anthropologists have been intrigued by this group from no later than the first half of the twentieth century (He & Faure, 2016; Wu & Situ, 2009). A popular and yet unsubstantiated legend has it that they were the various groups of aboriginals of southern China who escaped from the expansion of the northern dynasties by going into the floating world. What is beyond doubt, however, is that for centuries they "existed on the geographical and social fringe of Chinese society" (Hansson, 1996: 124) in very literal sense.

A closer look into the social dynamics in which the Tanka interacted with the landed society reveals more about being "outcasts" in imperial China. Their abysmal living conditions not only caught the attention from local officials, but also raised concern from the imperial court. As early as in Ming time (1368–1644), local gazettes had confirmed that the Tankas were: (1) registered in the *lijia* population managing and taxing system; (2) they were affected by the local landed interests; (3) some of the Tankas managed to integrate into the landed community (Ye, 1995: 83). However, despite being managed by the landed authorities, their marginal status in the society had not changed. The Qing court even issued an imperial edict to encourage the Tanka people to get landed and integrated. And yet, this edict "does not offer any suggestion as to how their inferior status had come into being" (Hansson, 1996: 127). It was perhaps the first time that the problem had reached the imperial level, but it remained a local issue, as the edict claims that "the Cantonese on shore are to blame, as old custom was said to enforce the discrimination against them [Tanka] and to be the cause of their drifting and restless life" (ibid.).

The very existence of the Tanka people has discredited an image of premodern China as a country without rural–urban distinction. The Tanka people are dependent on the city or town for their livelihood because they have no means for a sedentary life on land. Excluded from integrating into the city, they are a special example of urban outcasts before the modern time.

When the modern time did come with the opening up of trade ports after the First Opium War (1840–1842), new types of urban outcasts emerged. Take Shanghai as an example. Due to the devastating effects of serial civil wars and natural hazards, tens of thousands financially broken peasants from central China fled to the lower Yangtze River Delta and most of them took asylum in Shanghai.[5] During the Republican Era (1912–1949), the municipal government of Shanghai had made efforts to tackle this problem by supporting low cost housing projects known as Commoners' Village (Pinyin: *pingmin cun*. It is a euphemistic pun since *pinmin* means poor people). But the problem persisted as more refugees were coming. Typically, peasants from northern parts of the Jiangsu Province (note: Shanghai was a part of Jiangsu well until the end of 1920s) came in flocks travelling in their junks. These people were known as the "Subei people" (Pinyin: *subei ren*). Once arrived, they settled down along the creeks, e.g. the famous Suchow Creek, at the then outskirt of Shanghai.

The peculiar history of the Subei people in Shanghai is a specimen of outcasts in modern Chinese cities. As early as 1990, Emily Honig had noticed this type of urban exclusion in modern Shanghai (Honig, 1990). She found that both Chinese officials and western scholars "have overlooked a form of inequality that is perhaps most basic to China's largest urban centre, Shanghai, namely that based on native-place identification" (Honig, 1990: 273), and that "this pattern has persisted in the decades since 1949… because the problem has largely been ignored, neither fitting the officially recognized categories of class nor of ethnicity" (ibid.). To her, the Subei people forms a social category that is close to ethnicity despite the fact they were racially and culturally the same people as other social groups in Shanghai. Moreover, Lu was right to draw the conclusion that although these people had arrived in Shanghai, they were "not been 'accepted' by the metropolis", and that "physically in Shanghai" does not guarantee them to enjoy "facilities that a modern city can provide to its residents" (Lu, 1995: 589). Their lived in shacks or straw huts or even in the stranded junks, which is a condition reflective of their marginal status. In terms of collective psychology, "they hardly regarded themselves as 'urbanites'" as they were very much "outside of the city" (ibid.).

In the early 1950s, these shacks were exactly the target for demolishing by the revolutionary government in Shanghai. Perhaps due to the time lag between the years of editing and publication, the triumphant revolutionary tone created a rather ironic contrast to the reality in Shanghai

---

[5] For the discussion on natural hazards and social revolt in rural China, see for example: Perry, E. J. (1980) *Rebels and revolutionaries in North China: 1845–1945*. Stanford University Press.

when tens of thousands of fresh immigrants were forcibly turned back and driven out of the city in the few years around 1960. In the face of the new rural immigrants, the Chinese state decided to shut the door towards the city by instituting one of the most rigid tool of population movement governance, namely the *hukou* system. People are registered to a certain place, and this place is going to be indispensable in every step of his or her life course. Movement, either physically and socially, is put under severe control. Without people on the move, Chinese cities stopped to grow. It is no wonder that when it was again possible for foreigners to visit Shanghai in the late 1970s, many reported that they rediscovered a city that was frozen in the time capsule of the 1940s.

Beyond Etymology: Urban Village in the East and the West

English Translations of the chengzhongcun

The opening up of Chinese academia to the global scientific community, the application of foreign concepts and theories to phenomena in China has become a popular career move amongst Chinese urbanists who are eager to reconnect to the mostly Anglophone academia through publishing in English. This practice has been criticized by Tang Wing-Shing as "random conceptual appropriation" (Tang, 2014,). Surely it makes the cross-cultural communications much easier, but the pitfall is that the transplant of terms would disconnect the historical lineage of the cases. To de-context the milieu against which a term is coined is to subtract the true meaning of the term, hence would lead to confusion. Here I will check the "Urban Village" concept as an example to show how this term and the "*chengzhongcun*" are (mis-)used by some researches.

Despite the problematic reference, "Urban Village" was widely adopted as the English translation of the *chengzhongcun*. It conveys a clear image of the sharp contrast between what is urban and what is the rural other, in which the "cun" is the heterogeneity in the presumably homogeneous urban setting. Among the urban China researchers, a few had chose the term "*chengzhongcun*" (see: Tian, 2008; Zhang et al., 2003), while most others would prefer to "Urban Village" or "Villages-in-the-city". Occasionally researchers would check the applicability of the term in Chinese context, but have failed to provide in in-depth review in manifold meanings of the term "Urban Village" (Chung, 2010; Liu, 2019; Xie,

2005). Here below, I argue that the fundamental differences between the "Urban Village" and the *chengzhongcun* are deeply rooted in the history and culture of the respective societies.

Urban Village Across the Atlantic

As noted before, in his book *The Urban Villages*, Herbert J. Gans sorted the lower rent residential areas in American cities into two types: the place for first or second generation of immigrants and the disadvantaged areas of crime or exclusion. As to the first type, Gans referred to Little Italy, Ghetto and Black Belt before he first coined the term "urban village". To Gans, these areas are very important since they provide a space for immigrants to "adapt their non-urban institutions and cultures to the urban milieu". Those who benefited from this space are European immigrants as well as "Negro and Puerto Ricans". However, the second type, which Gans called "urban jungle", is in fact hardly distinguishable from the first in terms of population composition. Though Gans admitted that the two types are often intermingled with each other, but he was also aware of limit of the terms so he emphasized that the terms are by no means social or cultural definition but rather sort of description of the life quality, and "they are not ecological concepts, for neither in economic, demographic or physical terms do such areas resemble villages or jungles". Thus for Gans this term is clear and unambiguous. Importantly, for Gans, the term "slum" was problematic. He preferred to refer to the urban villages as "low rent housing".

The Gansian concept has had a unique etymological transformation in the decades following its birth. While Gans used the term in a sociological sense, it was introduced into urban planning before long. As early as in 1970, British urban sociologist Ray Pahl envisioned a type of modern community as an alternative to the modernistic city which was crystallized in the term "Urban Village" (Pahl, 1970). When John Connell wrote his paper *Urban Villages and Social Networks* in London, notwithstanding his awareness of Gans' work, his understanding of the urban village turned out to be very different (Connell, 1970). In Connell's terms, urban village does not have much to do with immigrants' enclaves, but rather formed a new line of urban planning. It was made public in an elaborated critique on the modernistic suburbanization (Taylor, 1973). Researchers have thoroughly shifted away from the Gansian usage (Bell & Jayne, 2004, etc.).

From then on, "Urban Village" has become one of the popular concepts in urban planning. In the US, it is closely associated with the New Urbanism movement; while in the UK, it reflects more of the up-middle class pursuit of ideal communities. Eventually, it was crystallized in 1998 by the Urban Village Forum:

> An urban village is a concept of a settlement which is small enough to create a community in the truest sense of the word - a group of people who support each other, but big enough to maintain a reasonable cross section of facilities. Walking determines the size - a 10 minute walk from one side to the other. To provide a sufficiently large population to maintain a range of community facilities all within a walkable distance means the density of development must be high. An urban village is densely developed in the centre, with town squares and key community focal points, density eases away from the centre, and the boundary of the village is marked by green space. (Urban Village Forum, 1998).

Some degree of nostalgia of English village life, which arguably characterized the mentality of the British middle class, is discernible. This ideal could easily remind the reader to the names like Ebenezer Howard. In practice, there are already several urban village projects carried out in the UK, Australia, the States and The Netherlands: all of them developed and highly urbanized countries. But why was the "urban village" ideal promoted in the more urbanized countries? Besides the classic myth that rural life is good while city life is bad, was there something left behind this "recycling" effort?

Clear enough that the recycling of the idea of a "village" is in every sense an innovation and urban creature, and should not be misunderstood as a retrospective movement. In order to understand that, it is necessary to zoom in to the scale of the city. Ideally, a city has no rate of urbanization as it is always one hundred percent urban. The line that divides the urbanized and un-urbanized is valid only when the scale goes beyond the city per se, and in practice it is often generated at the regional or national level. The control mechanism of the access to the city, i.e. the citizenship, is the defining fact of urbanity. In this light, the idea of urban village is not valid in developing countries not because the incapability of sustaining the rustic/pastoral community, but rather because the failure to guarantee equal citizenship in spite of the geographical location of the citizens.

Cities in developed countries are at a different stage than those in developing countries. Connell also referred to in his above mentioned paper the fact that England does not have a domestic rural to urban labour migration ever since the mid-nineteenth century (Connell, 1970). By contrast, the two most populated countries in the world, China and India, have not yet reached the point of 50% urbanization. To connect these different usages of the "urban village" with the Chinese informal settlement *chengzhongcun* would be very problematic and prone to faults. It is problematic because while the Chinese *chengzhongcun* is generated on the basis of rural village, it has little to do with the idyllic country life that the British Urban Village movement aspired to. It is prone to faults because the seemingly comparability could obscure fundamental causes.

CONCLUSION

In this chapter I have reviewed, from a historical perspective, the genesis of the city superiority against the countryside and the history of Chinese urban outcasts. These two points are vital to the theoretical framework of urban China studies. As the urban history of Europe has shown, the rise of the city is also a process whereby the city created institutional mechanisms to regulate its relationship with its others, whatever that may be. The Chinese city was neither merely the seat of a despotic governor of irrigation projects, nor a boundless community ruled as the village. It was only in the beginning of the twentieth century when very few cities and prime towns in China were granted the right of autonomous governance. The Chinese city entered the modern era carrying its legacy from the imperial. From the Tangka to Subei people, urban outcasts were never far from Chinese cities.

The socialist revolution since 1949 has essentially eliminated the urban outcasts problem in China (and the slum, of course), if only we could believe in what is proclaimed in official documents. Indeed, four decades into the economic reform since early 1980s, slum-like communities have never gained predominance in Chinese urban landscape. Compared to most of the developing countries, cities in China are neat, tidy and formal. The informal parts are hidden behind the walls and confined to some "corners". Defying to the mission of the socialist revolution, the reemergence of the urban outcasts and their communities is much, much more complicated. However, the contemporary situation should not be mistaken with that before the revolution, for the Chinese revolution has redefined the institutional framework that rules over the hundreds of millions of lives. Understanding this redefining process is crucial to the understanding of China's urban outcast problem. This will be addressed in the next chapter on the political economy of the *chengzhongcun*.

REFERENCES

Arrighi, G. (2007). *Adam Smith in Beijing: Lineages of the twenty-first century.* Verso.

Bell, D., & Jayne, M. (Eds.). (2004). *City of quarters: Urban villages in the contemporary city.* Ashgate.

Brundage, J. A. (1979). Review: Henri Pirenne: A biographical and intellectual study by Bryce Lyon. *Speculum, 54*(1), 174–176. https://doi.org/10.2307/2853026

Carter, H. (1983). *An introduction to urban historical geography.* E. Arnold.

Chung, H. (2010). Building an image of villages-in-the-city: A clarification of China's distinct urban spaces. *International Journal of Urban and Regional Research, 34*(2), 421–437. https://doi.org/10.1111/j.1468-2427.2010.00979.x

Connell, J. H. (1970). *Urban villages and social networks* (Occasional Paper No.11). Department of Geography, University College London.

Denecke, D., & Shaw, G. (Eds.). (1988). *Urban historical geography: Recent progress in Britain and Germany.* Cambridge University Press.

Entrikin, J. N. (1980). Robert Park's human ecology and human geography. *Annals of the Association of American Geographers, 70*(1), 43–58. https://doi.org/10.1111/j.1467-8306.1980.tb01296.x

Froeyman, A. (2004). *Max Webers 'Die Stadt' en de Gentse historiche school.* Masters' thesis of Ghent University. Available at http://www.ethesis.net/clio/clio_inhoud.htm [Accessed July 24, 2011].

Hansson, A. (1996). *Chinese outcasts: Discrimination and emancipation in late imperial China.* Brill.

He, X., & Faure, D. (2016). *The fisher folk of late imperial and modern China: An historical anthropology of boat-and-shed living.* Routledge.

Honig, E. (1990). Invisible inequalities: The status of Subei people in contemporary Shanghai. *The China Quarterly* (122), 273–292. https://doi.org/10.1017/S0305741000008791

Isin, E. (2002). *Being political: Genealogies of citizenship.* University of Minnesota Press.

Jacobs, J. (1984). *Cities and the wealth of nations: Principles of economic life.* Penguin Books Ltd.

Le Galès, P. (2002). *European cities: Social conflicts and governance.* Oxford University Press.

Liu, Y. T. (2019). Village in the city. In *The Wiley Blackwell encyclopedia of urban and regional studies*. Wiley Blackwell. https://doi.org/10.1002/978111856 8446.eurs0408

Lu, H. (1995). Creating urban outcasts: Shantytowns in Shanghai, 1920–1950. *Journal of Urban History, 21*(5), 563–596. https://doi.org/10.1177/009 614429502100501

Lyon, B. (1974). *Henri Pirenne: A biographical and intellectual study*. E. Story Scientia.

Morris, R. J., & Rodger, R. (Eds.). (1993). *The Victorian city: A reader in British urban history, 1820–1914*. Longman.

Mote, F. (1977). The transformation of Nanking, 1350–1400. In W. Skinner (Ed.), *The city in late imperial China* (pp. 102–105). Stanford University Press.

Myers, G. (2011). *African cities: Alternative visions of urban theory and practice*. Zed Books.

Pahl, R. E. (1970). *Spatial structure and social structure*. CES WP10. Centre for Environmental Studies.

Perry, E. J. (1980). *Rebels and revolutionaries in North China: 1845–1945*. Stanford University Press.

Pirenne, H. (1936). *Economic and social history of medieval Europe*. Kegan Paul, Trench, Trubner & Co., Ltd.

Pirenne, H. (1969). *Medieval cities: Their origins and the revival of trade*. Princeton University Press.

Pomeranz, K. (2001). *The great divergence: China, Europe, and the making of the modern world economy*. Princeton University Press.

Rowe, W. T. (1984). *Hankow: commerce and society in a Chinese city, 1796–1889*. Stanford University Press.

Skinner, W. (Ed.). (1977). *The city in late imperial China*. Stanford University Press.

Smith, A. (2007). *An inquiry into the nature and causes of the wealth of nations*. Harriman House.

Tang, W. S. (2014). Governing by the state: A study of literature on governing of Chinese mega-cities. In P. O. Berg & E. Bjoner (Eds.), *Branding Chinese mega-cities: Policies, practices and positioning* (pp. 42–63). Edward Elgar.

Tang, W. S. (2019a). Introduction: Urban China research is dead, long live urban China research. *Eurasian Geography and Economics, 60*(4), 369–375. https://doi.org/10.1080/15387216.2019.1699434

Tang, W. S. (2019b). Town-country relations in China: Back to basics. *Eurasian Geography and Economics, 60*(4), 455–485. https://doi.org/10.1080/153 87216.2019.1686407

Tang, W. S. (2021). Reframing urban China research: A critical introduction. In W. S. Tang & K. W. Chan (Eds.), *Urban China reframed: A critical appreciation* (pp. 1–16). Routledge.

Taylor, N. (1973). *The village in the city: Towards a new society.* Temple Smith.

Tian, L. (2008). The Chengzhongcun land market in China: Boon or bane?—A perspective on property rights. *International Journal of Urban and Regional Research, 32*(2), 282–304. https://doi.org/10.1111/j.1468-2427.2008.007 87.x

Urban Village Forum. (1998). *Urban villages: A concept for creating mixed-use urban developments on a sustainable scale* (2nd ed.). Urban Villages Forum.

Verhulst, A. (1999). *The rise of cities in North-West Europe.* Cambridge University Press.

Weber, M. (1951). *The religion of China: Confucianism and Taoism* (H. H. Gerth, Trans.). The Free Press.

Weber, M. (1968). The city: Non-legitimate domination-concepts and categories of the city. In G. Roth & C. Wittich (Eds.), *Economy and society: An outline of interpretive sociology* (Vol. 2). Bedminster Press Incorporation.

Wittfogel, K. S. (1957). *Oriental despotism: A comparative study of total power.* Yale University Press.

Wu, S., & Situ, S. (2009). Tangka research progress and a new perspective of study on cultural geography. *Tropical Geography, 29*(6), 583–587 [in Chinese].

Xie, Z. (2005). *The transition from village to urban community: A study of institution, policy and the urban village problem during the urbanization in China.* China Social Sciences Press [in Chinese].

Ye, X. (1995). Notes on the territorial connections of the Dan. In D. Faure & H. F. Siu (Eds.), *Down to earth: The territorial bond in South China.* Stanford University Press.

Zhang, L., Zhao, S. X. B., & Tian, J. P. (2003). Self-help in housing and Chengzhongcun in China's urbanization. *International Journal of Urban and Regional Research, 27*(4), 912–937. https://doi.org/10.1111/j.0309-1317. 2003.00491.x

CHAPTER 3

Housing and the Political Economy of Urban China

Abstract The *chengzhongcun* is a product of the unique political economic settings of post-reform China. This chapter begins with a discussion on the international legal frameworks that aimed to stimulate the awareness of the right to urban housing which, however, are unbinding and have to rely on grounded practices to get materialized. China's post-reform urban development poses a drastic twist from the Soviet legacy that it inherited in the immediate years following the founding of the People's Republic. Yet, the mechanisms of land and population governance are largely kept intact after the reform. Therefore, while the *chengzhongcun* is problematic in many ways and certainly very different from the Urban Village Movement in the UK and similar phenomena elsewhere, Him Chung's dystopian portrayal has missed out on its deep-rooted political economic causes.

Keywords Housing right · Hukou · Soviet · New Urbanism · Dystopianism

> *I see, long after A.D. 2000, cities laid out for ten to twenty million inhabitants, spread over enormous areas of country-side, with buildings that will dwarf the biggest of to-day's and notions of traffic and communication that we should regard as fantastic to the point of madness.* (Spengler, 1927: 101)

© The Author(s), under exclusive license to Springer Nature   41
Singapore Pte Ltd. 2022
Y. Ding, *Urban Informal Settlements*,
https://doi.org/10.1007/978-981-16-9202-4_3

INTRODUCTION

Although the urban development is a complicated matter, many urban China scholars tend to reduce the *chengzhongcun* as a question urban housing. Surely, for more than three decades the *chengzhongcun* has facilitated the Chinese city to partially solve the problem of shortage in affordable urban housing, particularly for the rural immigrants. Excluded by both the public redistribution regime and the speculative housing market, immigrants have few choices other that the *chengzhongcun*. Their right to urban housing is insecure and the mechanism to protect that right is ineffective even by the Chinese standard. One should question if they were intentionally kept in a state like that.

On the other hand, the *chengzhongcun* is often portrayed as the eyesore by city governments, real-estate developers, and even the general public. Consequently, this view leads some to conclude that the urban planning system was responsible for the social and environmental problems associated with the *chengzhongcun* (Chung, 2010). But can this problem be solved by an improved state of urban planning? Or, indeed, is the *chengzhongcun* actually a purely technical question of housing shortage?

Recently, Tang Wing-Shing has highlighted the methodological weakness in contemporary urban China studies, adding that "one must concentrate not simply on the most recent developments at the expense of the past. Dividing post-1949 China into two mutually exclusive pre- and post-reform periods is absolutely a hindrance to penetrating the reality. An historical approach to trace the developments over time is desperately needed, in addition to a spatial one deciphering the intricate interaction between China and the world" (Tang, 2021: 10). I concur with him, and would like to return to the basics of the right to urban housing, the elements of the Soviet legacy in China, so as to probe the political economy of the Chinese urban development.

THE RIGHT TO URBAN HOUSING

Pendulum Between Human Right and Civil Right

Housing right is a case whereby human rights and civil rights converge. The right to urban housing is tricky in the sense that while housing is the basic need for human habitation, it involves more than supplies to meet the needs. The affordability and accessibility of housing lie at the nexus of location, size, amenities, etc. The access to housing is embedded in the society, which organizes the production, distribution, and maintenance of housing resources. The recognition of housing rights as both a fundamental human right and a practical civil right is the first step towards the solution of urban housing problems.

As the world gets more urbanized than ever, a reconsideration of the right to urban housing is at stake. It may be argued that urbanity does have various degree of concessions according to the local standard, however, extreme conditions such as over-crowdedness, lack of sewage, lack of safe water supply, etc. were and are still hampering human development for hundreds of millions people. Should an urban life be defined according to the middle class lifestyle in the developed world, then the rate of global urbanization would be reduced sharply. The reality, of course, is that those people are struggling to make a living in spite of the precarious conditions of third world slums. Compared to livelihood, housing is perhaps a less urgent issue. Nonetheless, given the close association between human development indicators, such as health and education, and housing conditions, the right to housing should be uphold as a fundamental human right, and it is necessary to have a basic universal housing standard (see UN-Habitat, 2003).

On the other hand, urban housing is far more complicated than, for instance, rural housing, although by no means is rural housing something happens spontaneously or "naturally". To make urban housing work, prerequisites such as landownership, planning regulations, finance, supplies, etc. should be settled beforehand to secure the provision. Seeing from the point of view of human rights, it is no question that each and every human being should have the access to housing, but who has the access to urban housing and who hasn't, or who gets it in which way and why others can't do the same, etc. such are the questions that involve the civil right to housing.

The right to urban housing is the pendulum between human right and civil right. It may remind us of the famous catch phrase "the right to the city" from French philosopher Henri Lefebvre. Numerous works have been written on the basis of this concept. However, only a few, such as the Situationist Bill Brown, were able to criticize its groundlessness (Brown, 2006). Indeed, without the discussion on the preconditions and a clearly stated definition, "the right to the city" is no more than a hollow slogan. In India, slum residents chose to built their shacks along the railway not because the railway is their preferred means of transportation, but rather that the strips of land on both sides of the railway are owned

Fig. 3.1 Slum along a railway in India (*Source* Photo taken by the author on February 27, 2009, Kolkata, India)

by the government, therefore they could occupy it without the fear of being driven out by private land owners (Fig. 3.1). Recently, Carmalt has pointed out that in order to give human right a tangible grasp, there is no other way than have it situated and enacted (Carmalt, 2011). In line with him, and considering the supporting system of housing provision, I argue that urban housing is a human right primarily dependent on localized civil right.

Legal Framework

The right to housing is well acknowledged in international conventions, notably in the United Nations Housing Rights Programme. As early as in 1948, the *Universal Declaration of Human Rights* had proclaimed the right to housing as a basic human right (Article 25). Thereafter, in 1969, 1976 and 1986, it was repeatedly highlighted as a constitutive right to proper human habitation. For instance, in the *Declaration on Social Progress and Development* (1969), there were two articles specifically addressing the problem of housing provision:

Article 10
(f) The provision for all, particularly persons in low income groups and large families, of adequate housing and community services.

Article 18
(d) The adoption of measures to introduce, with the participation of the Government, low-cost housing programmes in both rural and urban areas.

With special attention being given to disadvantaged areas, it is kind of a precursor to the UN Millennium Development Goals. In terms of the legal responsibility, the *Declaration on the Right to Development* (1986) made it clear that "States should undertake, at the national level, all necessary measures for the realization of the right to...basic resources, education, health services, food, housing, employment and the fair distribution of income" (Article 8).

However, it is far more difficult implementing the international agreements in reality than making them. The UN-Habitat has compiled a set of national and international laws, regulations and bylaws that aimed to protect the housing right. However, in practice, the protection and provision depends on local and national level institutions, and almost no international organization could enforce the rule over member states. Take the European Union (EU) as an example. Although it is widely known for championing the welfare state policy, there is "no direct competence regarding issues of housing policy" at the EU level (Edgar et al., 2002: 18). It is a plain fact that not every member state is equally enthusiastic about it, since it has so much to do with the social and economic rights that are at the discretion of the government. As a matter of fact, "Following an action initiated by the UK, the [European] court [of Justice] confirmed that in the field of social policy only 'nonsignificant' actions - defined as those that do not interfere with policy arrangements of member states – can be legally executed by the EU" (ibid.). It is not likely that all member states would be willing to alienate their sovereign rights on social-economic issues to the Union.

Critiques on the Right to Urban Housing

Urban housing attracted the attention of social thinkers ever since the nineteenth century. Fredrick Engels, for example, criticized the Proud-honism, i.e. solving the problem of housing for the proletariat by making them "bourgeois" house-owners, for being reactionary. He pointed out that "the breeding places of disease, the infamous holes and cellars in which the capitalist mode of production confines our workers night after night, are not abolished; they are merely shifted elsewhere!" (Engels, 1872). While this was an early critique on the spatiality of Capitalism, lately reinterpreted by David Harvey, Engels might not have envisioned the global ramifications of urban housing policy. To Engels, the revolutionary force of the proletariat is able to solve the housing problem by itself.

Interesting enough, a century later, Bourdieu Bourdieu has criticized the housing market that sustained the "semi-detached dream" of the French middle class, to whom the whole process of *embourgeoisement* is a rather troubled path to follow. He pointed out that "because they find themselves drawn to live beyond their means, on credit, they discover the rigours of economic necessity almost as painfully as did the industrial workers of a different era" (Bourdieu, 2005: 186). In Post-war United States, middle class housing ownership became an integral part of the American Dream. Suburbanization and inner city urban renewal culminated during this period. The case of the West End in Boston and the Levittown of New Jersey, both studied by Herbert Gans, are representatives of the time. Indeed, it was the overheated American housing market that served as the harbinger of the 2008 financial crisis, the effects of which can still be felt as this line is being written.

In China, Chen Yingfang and her team have made great efforts in deepening the understanding of socio-political dynamics of urban development of Shanghai in the past two decades (Chen, 2009). Based on in-depth case studies, they revealed how the inner city gets redeveloped under the conditions that the compensation helped the residents to realize the improvement of living standard which they would not be able to achieve by themselves. In the meantime, outer villages are being transformed into conglomerated township residential areas to make room for industrial development. Against the background of the 2010 Shanghai EXPO, which bears the official motto "Better City, Better Life", it was the right time to raise an explicit criticism on the question of "whose city"

Shanghai actually is (Li et al., 2010). Buzz words such as green city or sustainability are the ethos of that exposition. However, rural immigrants have no place in an international event on the city, and *chengzhongcuns* are being demolished to make room for new boulevards leading to the EXPO site. Social justice in the urbanisation process is absent from the flamboyant stage in Shanghai, which is craving for being a truly global city (Chen et al., 2009).

THE SOVIET LEGACY

Background

Many scholars in urban China studies have labeled the current era as a "transitional" one. It is an undeniable fact that the profound transition is engulfing cities and towns even in the most remote corners of the country. The Chinese authority often reiterates that China is still in the "preliminary stage of socialism", and the development goal has been set as a "Socialism with Chinese Characteristics". Reintroducing market economy, it seems, is the means to achieve the goal. Thus, the era since the reform is transitional, and perhaps also exceptional. However, it was never made clear where the transition would lead to. Moreover, urban China studies seldom touch upon the period before the reform.

However, no matter how unpopular it is in present-day China, the Soviet legacy can not be simply discarded or erased from China's modern history. As late as in the mid-eighties Soviet theorists, Soviet urban geography was still being introduced to China (Dmitriev & Mezhevich, 1985; Kovalenko, 1984). It is not clear if these translated works have had any influence upon Chinese officials and scholars; after all, it was only in the late 1980s that the diplomatic relationship between China and the Soviet Union returned to a normal mode. Nonetheless, some of these works are quite interesting. Take Dmitriev and Mezhevich's book as an example. It is actually a quite readable book that contains serious exploratory discussions on the challenges of keeping up with evolving urban lifestyles rather than obsolete repetitions of Marxist dogmas (Dmitriev & Mezhevich, 1985: 71–92). They proposed to distinguish urban lifestyle, which is conventionally conceived as rooted in the city, from the urban lifestyle of the citizens. By breaking the nexus between urban environment and urban lifestyle, they not only echoed the official line of minimizing the divide between the city and the countryside, which is a given, but also explored the possibility of dispersed rather than conglomerated urbanism.

The history of Russian cities is relatively short, and its level of development is no comparison with its Western neighbours. "Ancient and medieval cities [of Russia] were, first of all, fortified places, consisting of a *kreml'*, surrounded by a moat or bank, and a *posad*. The *kreml'* was inhabited by the aristocracy and the *posad* by commoners and was used for commerce" (Parkins, 1953: 3). The level of urbanisation and industrialisation in Imperial Russia remained very low until before the October Revolution in 1917.[1] It is said that some members of the late nineteenth-century Russian intelligentsia even inquired Karl Marx whether Russia should take up the capitalist road in order to form a socialist society, or simply do so right upon the basis of rural communes, and to the later option Marx replied with conditional approval (Pallot & Shaw, 1981: 15). Eventually, the nature of Russia's level of development not only led to the political split between parties and sections, but also resulted in long and painful adjustments attempted to figure out a collective route plan for the newly born Soviet Union.

The Soviet urban planning system was hybridity of both Western urban planning theories and techniques and native practices. Notable early examples include the construction of St. Petersburg in the early eighteenth century. When it came to the early twentieth century, the Tsarist Russia was at the cross road and was in dire need to industrialise and urbanise. At that moment, Russian urban planners were rather unimpressed the condition of European cities which was far from desirable. Instead, new developments such as Ebenezer Howard's theory seemed all the more promising. Later on, the English "*Satellite Town*" concept as well as Le Corbusier's ideas were introduced to the Soviet Union in the early 1930s (Parkins, 1953: 23).

Despite the "anti-urban" sentiment that once grasped a part of the Russian society from imperial ministers (Stites, 1989) to peasant writers (Clark, 1985), the Soviet was determined to achieve "the long-term goal [...] to transform the existing rural settlements, villages, hamlets, and isolated farmsteads into small towns with the amenities and social structures of urban places" (French & Hamilton, 1979: 7). By the late

---

[1] For the discussion on urbanization in late Imperial Russia, and especially the relationship between rural immigrants and urbanites, see Bradley, J. (1985) *Muzhik and Muscovite: Urbanization in late imperial Russia*. University of California Press.

Fig. 3.2 A semi-deserted workers' club (front right) in remote area in China (*Source* Photo taken by the author on June 10, 2016, Anqing, China)

1970s, about two thirds of the citizens of the Soviet Union were urban dwellers (ibid.). The Soviet mode of urban development looked, at least at some point of the twentieth century history, quite attractive to those less-developed countries. Modeled in the Soviet style, you may even find a workers' club in remote rural areas in China (Fig. 3.2).

Soviet Planning and Its Problems

Scholars have widely noted the principles of planning in the Soviet Union (Bater, 1980: 27–31; Khazanov, 1998; Lewis & Rowland, 1969; Parkins, 1953: 51–55). The most prominent one is perhaps the mission to elimi- nate social inequalities through planning. As Underhill puts it, "equality, rather than liberty or diversity, has been a fundamental tenet of Soviet

planning and housing policy" (Underhill, 1990: 265). When it was translated into spatial terms, it aimed at "eliminating differences between the
city and the village" (Parkins, 1953).

Khrushchev was a key figure in the transformation of the Soviet city
as we knew it. After the industrialisation (through Five-Year Plans), the
WWII, and Stalin's rule, Khrushchev came up with a softened hand and
paid more attention to the living standard of citizens. He "pointed to
the need to raise living standards, arguing that this was the way to secure
the masses' commitment to socialism [...and] stress[-ed] the necessity of
catching up with and overtaking the greatest capitalist power, the United
States, both in production and living standards" (Pallot & Shaw, 1981:
20). He aimed to provide fair housing for the Soviet citizens. For most
of the time since Khrushchev's rule, Soviet citizens were secured with a
minimum of nine square meters housing space per person. The building
quality of some of the pre-fabricated blocks was, however, a different
matter. The mocked projects of *Khrushcheby*, "five-story houses of very
low quality construction, whose building was initiated under Khrushchev"
(Khazanov, 1998: 284), which were so-called to imitate the word for
slums in Russian: *trushcheby*.

The peculiar social-political conditions in the Soviet Union also created
special urban societies. Take suburbanisation as an example: While, in
Post-war United States, suburbanisation was characterised by middle class
suburban towns, such as the Levittowns, Lewis and Rowland noted
that "the formation of suburbs in the USSR is the result of a somewhat different process of suburbanization, namely, the growth of suburbs
has not been accompanied by a population decline in the central city"
(Lewis & Rowland, 1969: 788). The reason is perhaps the urbanisation
process in the Soviet Union was not as complete as in the States. Another
peculiar feature is the *agro-gorod*, which roughly reads as "rural cities".
The agricultural specialist Lazar Volin had noted that this Khrushchevian
ideal was not feasible to be applied to the whole country (Volin, 1955:
451), despite its success in Ukraine in the Pre-WWII years. He equally
pointed out that the financial "scissors", i.e. the Stalinist accumulation
policy favouring urban industry at the expense of rural agriculture, was
pertained in the Soviet Union (ibid.: 455). In general, the Soviet urban
community is different from the normal Western model.

In the Soviet period, the notion of community was more associated with
where people worked rather than where they lived. Industrial and other

enterprises served as additional social-welfare agencies which provided their employees with housing, health care, sporting facilities, recreation, nurseries and kindergartens, even with deficit foodstuffs, goods and services. (Khazanov, 1998: 277)

The Soviet system was constructed according to rational planning, so much so that the population movement was controlled and guided to suit the economic needs. In practice, "the *propiska* keeps the nation's capital relatively orderly and protected from huge waves of unemployed people in search of work", while in the meantime "workers are offered pay at 2.5 times normal pay, extra vacations, and the ability to retain access to their old apartments" should they wish to work in remote areas (Underhill, 1990: 266). With the aim of reducing regional inequality, however, the system arrived at the point that "to move horizontally in the USSR is to move vertically" (David Shipler, in Underhill, 1990), because the distribution of certain services at certain places was firmly controlled in an hierarchical manner.

The *propiska* acted as a kind of "domestic visa" for Soviet citizens. And it is after this system that the Chinese *hukou* system was conceived in the early 1950s. By the end of that decade and after the Great Leap Forward, however, the urbanisation in China came to a halt. The *hukou* system was officially promulgated in 1958 to control the free immigration to the city (see the next section).

The Soviet planning system also extends to the population growth. "The Soviet scholars held the notion that significant declines in the birth rate of developing nations could be attained through a high rate of employment among married women" (Mazur, 1968: 319). However, despite agreeing on the deterministic relationship between the economic base and social structure, many Western Marxists "oppose interventionist schemes designed to directly manipulate population variables" (McQuillan, 1982: 115).

The Soviet system had more problems than that. One of the widely acknowledged conflicts is that "between regional and sectoral interests" (Bater, 1980: 169; Underhill, 1990: 275). Take urban housing provision as an example, powerful enterprises would try to satisfy the need of their employees rather than waiting for the city planning office to address the problem. But the more fundamental challenge is the inherent contrast between social control and mobility. Tightly controlled Soviet

cities could easily suffocate creativity, which is vital to the social development, culture, and science. The lag in the development of informational
science was deemed as one of the reasons the Soviet Union irreversibly
lost its competitiveness (Castells, 1997: 5–68).

When Gorbachev came to power in the early 1980s, he brought
in manoeuvre unseen in the Soviet system by increasing "the diversity
and vitality of cities throughout the Soviet Union" (Underhill, 1990:
284). The *perestroika* policy was aimed to increase the vitality in the
Soviet system, so much so that "many American specialists" were even
being warned by the lure of "the methodology of centralised planning and the advantages of a government-managed economy" (Bocharov,
1991: 366). However, the reform was too difficult to control, let along
predict. "Urban society in Russia was least beset by problems when
totalitarian authority was at its strongest. When controls over urban
development and population movement collapsed in the face of rapid
urban-industrialization, an urban crisis of unparalleled dimensions took
hold" (Bater, 1980: 169), which, as we all know it, eventually cost the
very existence of the Union.

After the Soviet Union

Perhaps it was out of humility and prudence to claim that "geographers
in the Western world so far have paid remarkably little attention to their
socialist neighbours" (French & Hamilton, 1979: 3), but it is true that
"the Soviet experience in planned urban development stands out as both
different from, and of instruction to, Western society" (Bater, 1980: 170).
This argument is equally, if not more, true in the Chinese case. The differences between the Chinese reform and the Soviet *perestroika* will continue
to be an intriguing topic.

After the "Shock Therapy", Russian cities experienced changes that
proved the potentials of the *perestroika*. On the one hand, the aspiration
of the "Western way of life" is unashamed as shown in the burgeoning
advertisements that "demonstrate the possibility of choice in goods and
services" (Khazanov, 1998: 273–274). On the other hand, "the relative
prosperity of Moscow attracts not only the upwardly mobile, but also
those who have sunk to the bottom" (Khazanov, 1998: 278). Social
segregation is a logical outcome. Both of these two aspects are not
unfamiliar to Chinese cities after the reform.

Among the few scholars in urban China studies, Lu is one of first to point out that the Chinese *microdistrict* (Pinyin: *xiaoqu*) was modeled after the Soviet *microrayon* (Lu, 2006). However, her analysis on the Maoist period city overlooked the continuity of the Soviet planning thoughts in China. One of the questions that Lu failed to address is the ascendancy and predominance of Work Unit Compound (Pinyin: *danwei dayuan*) in China, a phenomenon almost non-existent in the Soviet society. Zhao has noted the influences from the Soviet Union in the early years of the Chinese Five-Year Plans (Zhao, 2007). She reviewed the adoption of many of the Soviet planning ideas before the Sino-Soviet split, and analyzed its influences on community planning with details (ibid.: 86–91, 128–148).

PLANNING OR POLITICAL ECONOMY: A DISCUSSION WITH HIM CHUNG

More Than Urban Planning or Design

More than 40 years ago, British sociologist Ray Pahl warned against the uncritical import of American sociological theory into British urban studies which ignored important differences between both societies (Pahl, 1970). While acknowledging a "common industrial-urbanism" that is shared by Britain and the US, he reminded his fellow British academics that "cultural differences are hard to define but crucial to an understanding of the situation. Hence I do not think that those sociologists, such as Herbert Gans, who do so much to popularize American subcultural styles among the sociologically unsophisticated, are as helpful as some of my British colleagues appear to think" (ibid.: 9).

In his contribution to *International Journal of Urban and Regional Research* (Chung, 2010), Him Chung reinvigorates Pahl's critique. This a welcome debate about the problem of transferring sociological concepts from one social setting to another. Focusing his critique on the application of the term "urban village" to "villages-in-the-city", Chung correctly explains that with the import of such concepts in Chinese social studies come along specific paradigms, values and perspectives which are not always fully taken into consideration. In his analysis, Chung explores the background of the urban village concept in Anglo-Saxon (or rather British) planning theory and assesses to what extent this theoretical framework is adequate to analyze *chengzhongcun*. He concludes that the British urban planning ideal of the "urban village" does not fit the social reality of the *chengzhongcun* but to a superficial level. In effect, he claims that whereas "the urban village model represents the search for a new, socially sustainable, model of urbanism, villages-in-the-city exhibit the urban ills that this movement is desperate to eliminate" (Chung, 2010: 435). Moreover, he concludes, we need more sophisticated tools to fully grasp the diversity of *chengzhongcun*. In particular, he suggests to make a distinction between "villages-in-the-city" and ethnic migrant enclaves. Both have developed as former rural settlements enclosed by an expanding city. Planning and land use regulations differ from the surrounding urban area which results in morphologically very distinct structures. However, whereas urban development of "villages-in-the-city" is driven by indigenous villagers, ethnically distinct rural migrants have taken over control of the process in ethnic migrant enclaves.

However, while Chung's intention is to clarify a number of prevalent misconceptions about *chengzhongcun* that might result from calling them "urban villages", his analysis remains incomplete and his arguments risk to obfuscate more than they clarify.

Chung situates the "urban villages" concept in the Urban Village Group, a planning movement which originated in the UK, alongside and in close interaction with North-America's New Urbanism movement (Thompson-Fawcett, 1998, 2003). While still a heterogeneous movement, its various proponents share an interest in preserving, restoring and even building new 'traditional' urban morphologies, with an emphasis on mixed use of space, the stimulation of social contacts and sense of community, and slow traffic. From a morphological viewpoint, Chung is right to refer to the British urban village literature to understand Chinese "villages-in-the-city": at a superficial level, both share a vernacular morphology, with a mixed and compact land use pattern (Franklin & Tait, 2002). Simultaneously, he correctly points out the different origins of "urban villages and "villages-in-the-city", the first being carefully designed at the drawing table, and the other the consequence of chaotic decision making procedures of indigenous villagers.

What he fails to consider, however, is the background to what Emily Talen has called "the social doctrine of New Urbanism" that is shared by its British counterpart, the Urban Villages (Talen, 1999). This social doctrine, focused around the idea of creating community through the built environment, was born out of one of the most pertinent critiques of Post-war modernist urban redevelopment (Connell, 1970).

Urban scholars in particular have voiced ferocious critique against the neglect of the social in modernist urban planning. Seminal works like Jane Jacobs' *Death and Life of Great American Cities* and Herbert Gans' *The Urban Villagers* or, in Britain, Young and Willmott's work on East London (see: Gans, 1962; Jacobs, 1961; Young & Willmott, 1957) undermined the credibility of the modernist *tabula rasa* approach to inner cities. They pointed to the lack of attention for existing social structures that characterized modernist attempts to build a new society. Indeed, modernist urban development was not only criticised for its inability to support community development through the built environment, but was even blamed for disrupting existing community structures by demolishing the old urban tissue. Planning visionaries such as quickly absorbed these critiques and developed sensitivity to smaller scale, vernacular designs (Duany & Talen, 2002; Krier, 1998). Out of their experiments stemmed a sort of "post-modernist" design movement, which in the 1990s formalized into the New Urbanism movement in the US and the Urban Village Group in the UK.

However, this strand of post-modernist urban planning theory only selectively borrowed from American social scientists' anti-modernist critique. Most forcefully ignored is their attack on the dystopian modernist imagination of the slum. Modernism largely developed as a reaction to the social foes of the nineteenth century inner city in Europe and America. The inner city slum, was considered an unhealthy, unjust, socially and morally downgrading environment, not very much unlike Chung's view on the *chengzhongcun*. Modernists addressed this slum problem with fervour and little distinction: wherever rundown nineteenth century working class housing was found, it had to be razed to the ground and make way for integral modern redevelopment projects. It was to this indiscriminately dystopian view on deprived inner city communities that urban sociologists reacted.

As noted before, Herbert J. Gans chose to study the Boston West End, commonly denoted by planners as a slum ready for demolition and redevelopment. He set out to describe its social structure in detail and to investigate without prejudice "the nature and dynamics of working- and lower class society and culture, and the impact of redevelopment" (Gans, 1962: XI).

Indeed, it was Gans who coined the term "urban village", but with an utterly different meaning than the one proposed by the "Urban Village Group". Gans used the term to denote a particular type of slum area.

Here, non-urban immigrants, having moved to the city, slowly adapt their traditions of communal village life to the mores of the city. While making clear he had no intention to romanticize the slum, he effectively succeeded in undermining the largely dystopian image urban planners held about the West End. Describing the social ties, shared norms and values, and habits of the area, he revealed how, although local culture differed strongly from that of middle class planners, it was "by and large a good place to live" (Gans, 1962: 16). The lesson of the study was that planners should look for what residents really need before drawing plans (Gans, 1969). In his analysis, the urban village appeared as a crucial context for working class survival strategies which were disrupted by the radical urban renewal of the neighbourhood.

Of course, Gans' analysis cannot be directly translated to the study of *chengzhongcun*. As Chung demonstrated with the British Urban Village literature, a transfer of Gans' urban village concept should proceed with care and we should indicate in detail where and under which conditions such a transfer would be justified. Gans' study of Italian immigrants in the twentieth century Boston West End is very particular, and it is hard to imagine comparable cases in present-day China. However, we identify two instances in which his analysis of an American "urban village" might prove inspirational for present day studies of the *chengzhongcun*.

First, Gans' urban village concept urges to move beyond crude and derogatory categorizations of urban areas, and to look for the actually existing social life in the areas concerned. Like the West End, *chengzhongcun* are too often considered 'bad places to live' on the basis of morphological characteristics alone. This opinion is not always shared by the residents. For example, the popular historian Gilda O'Nell documented the vivid living space of the "cockney London" of the traditionally deemed undesirable of the East End (O'Nell, 1999). In a study on poverty in Nanjing, researchers could show that levels of satisfaction towards the residential environment were relatively high in *chengzhongcun* (Babar & Kesteloot, 2009).

Moreover, Gans' ethnographic analysis of the everyday life experiences of residents could prove a crucial method to refine Chung's analysis of the diversity of *chengzhongcun*. Chung bases his distinction between "villages-in-the-city" and ethnic migrant enclaves upon the social and economic dominance of either indigenous villagers or an ethnically homogeneous migrant group, referring for the latter to the emblematic Zhejiang village in Beijing. He did not explore, however, how these patterns of dominance and solidarity had developed in particular places, and what assets are being deployed to maintain them. Such an approach would probably have revealed Zhejiang village as a very particular example of a migrant enclave (Zhang, 2001).

The Political Economy of Urban Inequality

Chung's analysis of the origins of *chengzhongcun* implies it was a planning failure. This leads him to put unsustainable hopes on a more efficient and effective planning system to "solve the problem" of *chengzhongcun*. His focus on spatial planning has blinded him for the wider political economy in which *chengzhongcun* originate. He explains "villages-in-the-city" by the failure to "integrate the new territories into the existing, urban-based, planning system" in expanding cities and by the fact that "this deficiency has attracted non-local people, i.e. migrant workers who live in cities, to develop their settlements in areas where planning and land-use prescriptions are not efficiently implemented" (Chung, 2010: 426).

This statement seems right at first sight. It is widely known that the dual system of land ownership in China, with different regulations for urban and rural land, has created difficulties for a coherent policy design and for the integration of rural land in the urban planning system. But this statement is based on the prescription that the spatial planning and policy system is meant to be equal and inclusive to both urban and rural parts of space and society. In other words, Chung's contribution preconceives the Chinese planning and land use regulation system as one that aims to bring urbanization and modernization to both the city and the countryside, and hence diminish the urban–rural gap.

While this representation indeed reflects the official goals of the Socialist planning era (Knight & Song, 1999), it neglects the fact that urban–rural polarization is part and parcel of the Chinese model of economic growth. The key-element in this political economy of urbanization is not spatial planning, but the *hukou* system which differentiates between a rural and an urban population register. A review of the curious history of the *hukou* system reveals its continued importance in the Chinese political economic system and explains why referring to *chengzhongcun* as a planning failure is overly naive.

The *hukou* system was ratified in 1958 as a means to check "blind" rural–urban migration in the early years of state socialism (Cheng &

Selden, 1994; Solinger, 1999). In the absence of a labour market, a planned economy needs population mobility control as a means to allocate labour to the spatially fixed means of production. The *hukou* - like the *propiska* in the Soviet Union - fixed the people in their place of registration and thus in the city or in the countryside, and warranted the right amount of labour force in industry and services on the one hand and agriculture on the other hand. The *hukou* does not only ascribe people to a certain place or area, but de facto also to a certain activity (agricultural in the countryside, non-agricultural in the city). In addition, a *hukou* entitles the bearer to specific consumption rights. While the holders of a rural *hukou* are supposed to be self sufficient as they have access to agricultural land and live in villages, urban *hukou* holders are supplied with housing, food and collective consumption goods and services such as child care, health care, cultural activities, etc. by their production units (Lu, 2004). Such services are often absent or insignificant in the rural areas.

As a crucial instrument for economic management in a planned society, the *hukou* system curiously remained in place after the 1979 reform that abandoned economic planning and introduced labour and housing markets. To facilitate control, the state has partitioned the country into urban and rural spaces and controlled the movement between the two; and in so doing, the state has established the spatial pre-conditions of surveillance, thereby reproducing its power and domination. However, *hukou* is no longer used for mobility control. In 1984 the state accepted rural migrants to settle in the cities and work there as far as they were able to provide for their own means of existence, including food, housing and medical care. Today, the *hukou* system is applied as a powerful instrument to manage the distribution of social rights. Like national citizenship in Western countries, the *hukou* system enables local governments to import "labour but not people" (Castles, 2006: 760). While allowing for the influx of labour, it exempts local governments from the costs of providing rural labour migrants with access to the social rights (including privileged access to social housing) urban residents enjoy. The *hukou* system deeply affected urban housing in China, even after the reform has lessened the importance of *hukou* (Bian & Logan, 1996). A further analysis reveals that the "winner" of the Chinese urban housing reform is the same group already favoured under the *hukou* system (Logan et al., 2010).

In the absence of access to state or company housing, rural immigrants are dependent upon private housing markets. The informal, often substandard but relatively affordable housing supply in *chengzhongcun* offers the non-urban masses a roof at close proximity to their places of employment (Chan et al., 2003; Wang et al., 2009; Zhang et al., 2003). The existence of *chengzhongcun* allows keeping wages down while simultaneously absolving city governments from the obligation to provide housing on nationalized urban land (McGee & Lin, 2007). Clearly, even a more powerful spatial planning system will not rid Chinese cities of *chengzhongcun*; they are at present an indispensable cog in the Chinese economic system.

The Way Out of the Chengzhongcun

Chung's critical analysis of the background of the Urban Village concept is important as there is indeed a danger of importing a concept without its societal context which might result in misconceiving, rather than clarifying the subject under scrutiny. His overly negative appreciation of *chengzhongcun* and belief that a stronger spatial planning approach would solve the problems might have been misplaced. Recently, there have been considerable attempts by urban planning organs to "deal with" *chengzhongcun*, strongly pushed by entrepreneurial city governments and a corporate real estate sector eager to grab and redevelop land in relatively central locations. This strategy goes so far that even some ordinary urban poor communities such as former industrial sub-district could be categorized as *chengzhongcun*. Interestingly, the official redevelopment motto is echoed in popular discourses biding goodbye to *chengzhongcun* while little critical thinking is produced. To this kind of modernist *tabula rasa* politics, the bleak picture that is often painted of *chengzhongcun* on the basis of their dilapidated structures serves as a welcome justification.

Like the planning discourse on *chengzhongcun*, these operations take little notion of the people who live there. While native villagers could still manage to articulate their interests, most of the immigrants have no title to the land or the house they rent, and remain voiceless against the violence afflicted upon them. Driven from their houses, they remain devoid of urban citizenship and hence dependent upon informal housing. Instead of improving their livelihood, *chengzhongcun* redevelopment is more likely to turn them into "redevelopment refugees", fleeing from one demolished *chengzhongcun* to another. Meanwhile, they are left disempowered as even long-established social networks and locally embedded livelihood strategies are disrupted.

Gans' urban village tradition of ethnographic neighbourhood exploration might prove an important source of inspiration, as it addressed fairly similar issues half a century ago. Such an ethnographic analysis of *chengzhongcun* will not only reveal the way social structures are maintained and reproduced, but will probably also reveal how these social structures are crucial for their residents to sustain certain essential livelihood strategies. Whereas middle class planners would interpret certain behaviours as signals of typical *chengzhongcun* deviance, it might well be behaviour which is highly adapted to the social position these residents find themselves in. It would, in any case, lead to a more nuanced understanding and appreciation of *chengzhongcun* as urban neighbourhoods. It will reveal how *chengzhongcun* are not only places of exclusion, but also act as the stepping stone for integration of newcomers to the city (Bach, 2010).

CONCLUSION

I started this chapter with the discussion on the housing right and ended with the political economy analysis of the *chengzhongcun*. Having put the *chengzhongcun* into perspective, it may be deemed as the space of transition. It harbours the village and immigrants as the city expands, and as China turns from planned economy to market economy, or "Socialism with Chinese Characteristics". The Soviet Union had made an example in tackling the rural–urban divide, and its policies had left deep imprints in China. However, ever since the Sino-Soviet split, China has been pushing its own ways ahead.

Him Chung was mistaken to blame the problems of the *chengzhongcun* on the fallacy of the planning system. Quite on the contrary, it is a logic outcome when the planning system was abolished. The Chinese reform was kicked off roughly at the time when the Neo-liberalism became the dominant economy policy. Market is the key molding force of the Chinese urban landscape in the last four decades, although some remnants from the Socialist era are still in effect, the *hukou* system being one of them. In order to figure out the policy linkage between the Chinese system and that of the Soviet Union, I have reviewed the urban policy of the later. It may be rightfully concluded that this peculiar hybridity of market force and Socialist policy engendered the *chengzhongcun* and determined the lives of hundreds of thousands of Chinese people. In

Li, L., Li, S., & Chen, Y. (2010). Better city, better life, but for whom? The *hukou* and resident card system and the consequential citizenship stratification in Shanghai. *City, Culture and Society, 1*(1), 145–154. https://doi.org/10.1016/j.ccs.2010.09.003

Logan, J. R., Fang, Y. P., & Zhang, Z. X. (2010). The winners in China's urban housing reform. *Housing Studies, 25*(1), 101–117. https://doi.org/10.1080/02673030903240660

Lu, D. (2006). *Remaking Chinese urban form: Moderninty, scarcity and space 1949–2005.* Routledge.

Lu, Y. (2004). *Chaoyue Hukou: Jiedu Zhongguo Huji Zhidu* [Beyond hukou: China's hukou registration system explained]. Chinese Social Science Press [in Chinese].

Mazur, P. (1968). Birth control and regional differentials in the Soviet Union. *Population Studies, 22*(3), 319–333.

McGee, T. G., & Lin, G. C. S. (2007). Representing the urbanization in China: Official and unofficial readings of the urban process. In G. C. S. Lin, J. P. Wu, T. G. McGee, M. Wang, & A. Marton (Eds.), *China's Urban Space: Development under market socialism* (pp. 53–73). Routledge.

McQuillan, K. (1982). On the development of Marxist theories of population. *Canadian Studies in Population, 9,* 109–116.

O'Neill, G. (1999). *My east end: Memories of life in Cockney London.* Penguin.

Pahl, R. E. (1970). *Spatial structure and social structure.* CES WP10. Centre for Environmental Studies.

Pallot, J., & Shaw, D. J. B. (1981). *Planning in the Soviet Union.* Croom Helm Ltd.

Parkins, M. F. (1953). *City planning in Soviet Russia.* University of Chicago Press.

Solinger, D. J. (1999). Demolishing partitions: Back to beginnings in the cities? *The China Quarterly, 159,* 629–639.https://doi.org/10.1017/S030557410 00003386

Spengler, O. (1927). *The decline of the west* (C. F. Atkinson, Trans.). Alfred A. Knopf.

Stites, R. (1989). *Revolutionary dreams: Utopian vision and experimental life in the Russian revolution.* Oxford University Press.

Talen, E. (1999). Sense of community and neighbourhood form: An assessment of the social doctrine of New Urbanism. *Urban Studies, 36*(8), 1361–1379. https://doi.org/10.1080/0042098993033

Tang, W. S. (2021). Reframing urban China research: A critical introduction. In W. S. Tang & K. W. Chan (Eds.), *Urban China reframed: A critical appreciation* (pp. 1–16). Routledge.

Thompson-Fawcett, M. M. (1998). Leon Krier and the organic revival within urban policy and practice. *Planning Perspectives, 13*(2), 167–194. https://doi.org/10.1080/026654398364518

Thompson-Fawcett, M. M. (2003). A new urbanist diffusion network: The Americo-European connection. *Built Environment, 29*(3), 253–270. https://doi.org/10.2148/benv.29.3.253.54283

Underhill, J. A. (1990). Soviet new towns, planning and national urban policy: Shaping the face of Soviet cities. *The Town Planning Review, 61*(3), 263–285.

UN-Habitat. (2003). *Developing a set of indicators to monitor the full and progressive realisation of the human right to adequate housing.* https://www.un.org/ruleoflaw/blog/document/monitoring-housing-rights-developing-a-set-of-indicators-to-monitor-the-full-and-progressive-realisation-of-the-human-right-to-adequate-housing/. Accessed November 10, 2011.

Volin, L. (1955). Khrushchev's economic neo-stalinism. *The American Slavic and East European Review, 14*(4), 445–464.

Wang, Y. P., Wang, Y. L., & Wu, J. S. (2009). Urbanization and informal development in China: Urban villages in Shenzhen. *International Journal of Urban and Regional Research, 33*(4), 957–973. https://doi.org/10.1111/j.1468-2427.2009.00891.x

Young, M., & Willmott, P. (1957). *Family and Kinship in East London.* Routledge & Kegan Paul.

Zhang, L. (2001). *Strangers in the city: Reconfiguration of space, power, and social networks within China's floating population.* Stanford University Press.

Zhang, L., Zhao, S. X. B., & Tian, J. P. (2003). Self-help in housing and Chengzhongcun in China's urbanization. *International Journal of Urban and Regional Research, 27*(4), 912–937. https://doi.org/10.1111/j.0309-1317.2003.00491.x

Zhao, C. L. (2007) *Socio-spatial transformation in Mao's China: Settlement planning and dwelling architecture revisited (1950s-1970s)* (Doctoral dissertation at Department of Architecture). Urbanism and Spatial Planning, KU Leuven.

CHAPTER 4

Chengzhongcun and Its Residents: Empirical Findings

Abstract How valid are those dystopian portrayals of the *chengzhongcun*? And who are the people of the *chengzhongcun*? This chapter presents a survey of two *chengzhongcuns* in Shanghai and Hefei, both located in eastern China, that was carried out in 2009. The aim was to probe the *chengzhongcun* residents' view on various issues in and beyond their community. The results show that the *chengzhongcun* is a very diverse community, and people have different living conditions as well as different viewpoints. Far from the stereotype of a dull, passive, and desperate community, it is vibrant and dynamic, full of people moving to take the advantages of this rural niche in the urban world. In spite of the great resilience of the *chengzhongcun* residents, their chance of getting integrated into the city is impeded by several constraints. Income and education are among the most important ones, but they are secondary to hukou, the Chinese domestic citizenship system.

Keywords Survey · Hukou · Migrants · Urban-rural dichotomy · cheng-cum-xiang

> *[The chengzhongcun is] even worse than rural villages!*
> (*chengzhongcun* resident in Shanghai 2009)

© The Author(s), under exclusive license to Springer Nature
Singapore Pte Ltd. 2022
Y. Ding, *Urban Informal Settlements*,
https://doi.org/10.1007/978-981-16-9202-4_4

INTRODUCTION

Having noted the resurgence of urban outcasts in Chinese cities as a historical phenomenon in previous chapters, and analyzed the political economy milieu against which informal urban settlements develop, the next logical scale would be to zoom in upon the *chengzhongcun*. The environment of the *chengzhongcun* is said to be uninviting if not miserable. It's not uncommon to find people, even counting scholars, who hold very negative view on the *chengzhongcun* and tend to interpret it as "urban ills" awaiting elimination (Chung, 2010: 435). However, how valid are those descriptions? Who, after all, are the people of the *chengzhongcun*? How do they think of the environment they live in? What are their views on the movement known as urbanisation?

I took these questions to the fields at the late 2000s and early 2010s. Through long term observations, and after consulting with some leading urban planners, I organized a survey in two cities, namely Shanghai (上海) and Hefei (合肥), in June–July 2009.[1] These two cities are located in eastern China, but they are at rather different stages of urban development (Fig. 4.1). While Shanghai is China's financial centre and one of its "first tier" metropolises, Hefei is but a provincial city. According to the Sixth National Population Census of China (NPCC) in 2010, Shanghai had a population of more than 23 million, whereas for Hefei it was about 5.7 million.

Nonetheless, Hefei, capital city of Anhui Province, was one of the fastest growing cities in China in the last two decades. In 2014, Anhui was included in a national plan aiming at enhancing regional integration of the Yangtze River Delta (YRD), which also included Shanghai and the neighbouring Jiangsu and Zhejiang Provinces. Between 2010 and 2020, Hefei had almost doubled its population and reached nearly 9.4 million. By comparison, Shanghai gained just about 1.5 million during the same period.

Therefore, this study will not only shed light on an understudied Chinese city undergoing breakneck growth, but also probe the diverse

[1] This survey, titled *Social Empowerment and Spatial Segregation with focus on Chinese 'Village in Cities'*, received financial support from the Foundation for Urban and Regional Studies (FURS. Now known as the IJURR Foundation). See: https://www.ijurr.org/ijurr-foundation/foundation-for-urban-and-regional-studies-ijurr-foundation-initiatives/research-grants-1995-2014/ (accessed September 10 2021).

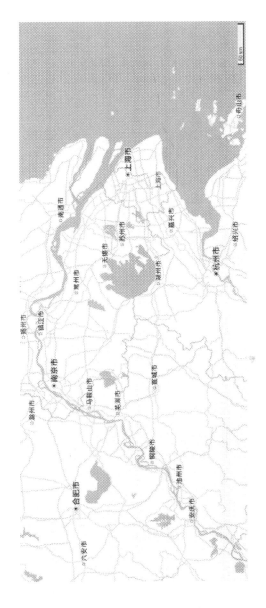

Fig. 4.1 Survey Sites: Shanghai and Hefei in Eastern China (*Source* https://map.tianditu.gov.cn/, accessed August 25, 2021)

contexts in which *chengzhongcuns* exist and the potential effects they would cause. Exact survey sites were selected from a large pool of similar *chengzhongcuns* in these two cities. The empirical findings as well as some of the first person observations are presented here below in this chapter. Statistical models have also been used to test hypotheses regarding the social-economic profile of the *chengzhongcuns* residents and their perceptions.

BACKGROUND AND IMPLEMENTATION OF THE SURVEY

Background Information

Social sciences were introduced into China in the early twentieth century. In the late 1910s, Sidney D. Gamble (1890–1968), an American Christian missionary, was probably the first to carry out a modern social survey in a Chinese city. His brilliant work on the livelihood of Peking (Beijing) households remains a classic (Gamble, 2011. First published in 1921). Major cities such as Beijing and Shanghai provided were both the dissemination hub for the ideas and techniques of doing surveys and the breeding ground for dire social crises. Tao Menghe, a London School of Economics (LSE) trained sociologist, founded the Institute for Social Surveys in Peking in the late 1920s. Social surveys became more commonly adopted by Chinese officials, intellectuals, and revolutionaries. They began to carry out surveys in cities and environs, and among manufacture workers, miners, railway workers and, of course, peasants, for whom Mao Zedong famously wrote *The Report on Hunan Peasant Movement* (Pinyin: Hunan nongmin yundong kaocha baogao) in 1927. In Shanghai, where the Communist Party of China (CPC) was founded in 1921, the plight of urban working class and the outcasts was the vividly captured by Leftists films producers such as Yuan Muzhi (1909–1978). Fei Hsiao-tung, who made a doctoral study on rural economics in the Yangtze River Delta (YRD) at the LSE in 1938, was among the most renowned sociologists in the decades to come.

Shacks formed a ring around the urban nuclei composed of foreign settlements and the old Chinese town. It is no wonder that Lu also included the distribution map of slum areas taken from *The Transitions of Shanty Towns in Shanghai* in his paper on outcasts in Republican Era Shanghai (Lu, 1995). Yet, besides some rather general descriptions, the 1962 pamphlet provides little detail on the actual living conditions and livelihoods of shanty town residents on the eve of and shortly after the revolution. That was, perhaps, too obvious for the contemporary authors and readers to merit documentation and demonstration in a propaganda material.

It should be noted here that district (comparable to borough) level administrative boundaries in Shanghai have undergone several rounds of adjustments throughout the last century. Nowadays, the archives related to suburban areas of Shanghai from the 1950s are scattered and stored in different district level archives. For instance, the former Xijiao (literally, western suburb) District had long been dismantled and partly merged into present day Minhang District (formerly Shanghai County). The Minhang District Archive (MHDA) keeps a dossier titled "Documents Related to Demolition of Shanty Towns along the Suzhou Creek" (MHDA51-2-587 1953). Among documents and maps, it contains 17 registration cards used in a "Household Survey for Dismantlement of Endangered Shacks along the Suchow Creek in Beixinjing Town" [Pinyin: chaichu beixinjing zhen yan wusongjiang weixian pengwu fen hu diaochabiao] from September 1953, which help to shed some light on the housing conditions and livelihood of the residents in the said shanty area.

Although the time their had been staying in the Beixinjing shanty town varies, the majority of the head of households came from Jiangsu Province (14 out of 17. The other 3 respondents left the column blank). To be specific, they came from Yancheng, Taizhou, Funing, and Dongtai, all of them located in the so-called "subei" (literally, northern Jiangsu) region. The popular means for livelihood include working as lumper, running fruit stalls, and letting a part of the shacks out.

Take household No.6 as an example (Fig. 4.2). It registered a man aged 29 working as a lumper. He was an immigrant from Jiangsu Province and had been living in No. 212, Beidi Road since 1941. He had a wife and a child to support. As a compensation for the demolition of his shack, he was offered a subsidy of 400,000 Yuan (before the monetary reform in the same year). That roughly equals half of the annual income of an average worker.[2] The card did not record, however, the address of his new home or his employment after shanty town clearances. In a more likely than

---

[2] See the *Shanghai Gazetteer of Labour*, Shanghai Academy of Social Sciences Publishing House, for the average annual income of a worker in 1953, available at: http://www.shtong.gov.cn/node2/node2245/node67474/node67481/node67548/node67562/userobject1ai64579.html [accessed November 2011].

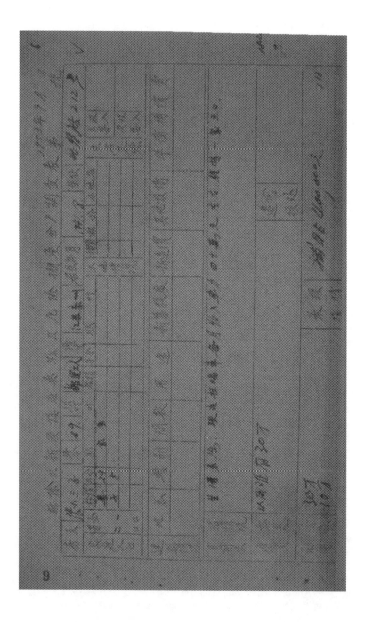

Fig. 4.2 Profile of a shanty town household in 1953 (*Source* Minhang District Archive (MHDA), Shanghai, China)

not scenario, he would have been recruited to one of the state-owned or collective-owned enterprises.

Other archives include proportions of agricultural land use in suburban areas. Taking Huacao Township of Xinjing Disctrict (dissolved in 1956 and merged into Xijiao Disctrict) as an example, the total arable land was 13,883 Mu (c. 926 hectares) in 1956, of which "watered field" is only 4601 Mu. For the rest "dry field", "permanent" and "non-permanent" vegetable growing land account for 7,151 Mu, or 77% (MHDA57-2-100 1956). It is perhaps unsurprising that the rural area in the vicinity of Shanghai was far from being merely rice paddies. Rather, villagers living there primarily engaged themselves in the supply of vegetables to the nearby metropolis. By taking part in this division of labour, these villager were already half-urban, or indeed, suburban in the early 1950s.

One of these villages is *Lujiayan* (陆家堰).[3] As a matter of fact, the fate of the Lujiayan *chengzhongcun* once experienced a curious twist when its surrounding area was transferred from under rural administration to urban in 1957 (MHDA57-1-63 1958). One of the reasons provided by Shanghai Civil Affairs Bureau to the People's Committee of Shanghai Municipality for the proposed transfer was that the land use characters (Pinyin: *tudi xingzhi*) and residents' employment statuses (Pinyin: *jumin chengfen*) had changed due to the fact that a large amount of arable land had been taken by two companies to store coal and timber (Fig. 4.3). Yet, the economic recovery in the 1950s was not smooth. When, during the first Five Year Plan (1953–1957) it was the standard practice for the city to provide employment to villagers whose land and house had been expropriated for urban and industrial development by the government, this practice was in effective suspended since early 1958. In stead, the new policy aimed to relocate the landless peasants into other and further suburban villages (MHDA57-2-204 1958). That, of course, was a precursor to the de-urbanisation movement during 1960–1962 when tens of thousands of recent immigrants were "persuaded" to voluntarily go back to the countryside. Urbanisation was halted in China and never recovered until after the reform.

Little is known of the subsequent developments, if any, taking place after its status change. When I first visited *Lujiayan* in early 2009, there were still tiny remnant patches of arable land, now used for cultivating

[3] Also written as 陆家埝, which reads as *Lujianian* in pinyin.

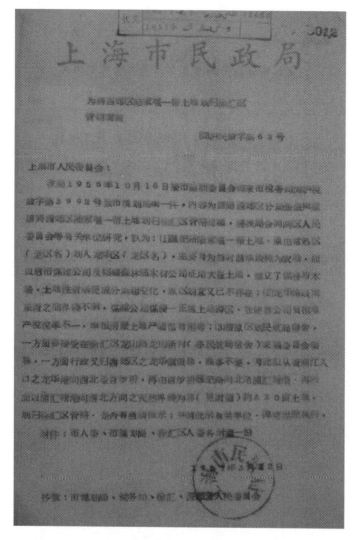

Fig. 4.3 Proposal on transferring Lujiayan to under urban administration, 1957 (*Source* Minhang District Archive (MHDA), Shanghai, China)

vegetables. The situation was same in the near by *Sanjiali* (三家里) *chengzhongcun*. At that time, the duo *chengzhongcuns*, Lujiayan-Sanjiali (below as LJY-SJL), were facing demolition to make room for development ahead of the EXPO Shanghai 2010. The Shanghai municipality and the Chinese government was determined to use this mega-event, which bore an official motto "Better City, Better Life", to make a strong case for urbanism.

The seat of the capital city of Anhui Province was moved to Hefei in 1952. However, for the next half century, it remained a medium sized inland city due to lack of investment. Economy in Anhui was predominantly agricultural, and Hefei was not on the trunk line of either the railway network or waterways. Urban development only took off in the second half of the 2000s.

Survey Sites in Shanghai and Hefei

It can be argued that the majority of English publications on the *chengzhongcun* are geographically focused in the Pearl River Delta (PRD). In fact, much like the Dharavi of Mumbai, or Rocinha of Rio de Janeiro, there have been also some "star" *chengzhongcuns* in the PRD that attract in-proportionally more researchers. During the preparatory stage, I visited Shenzhen and Guangzhou in 2007, and I found that the residents of the star *chengzhongcuns* are indifferent to (foreign) researchers, and this lead me to doubt if they had already been over-studied. I suspect they were too accustomed to the questions a researcher might raise.

On the other hand, up until the time I did my survey, there were very few publications based on fieldwork about *chengzhongcuns* in Shanghai. Actually, during the several interviews I had with expert urban planners and urban historians of Shanghai in 2009, they openly denied the existence of *chengzhongcuns* in Shanghai, believing that the municipal governance of Shanghai is good enough to avoid them.

I chose the other city, Hefei, not only because familiarity as it is my home city, but also because it stands as a contrast case to Shanghai. Local researchers had done some studies on the conditions and redevelopment projects of *chengzhongcuns* in Hefei (Ye, 2005; Ye & Xu, 2008; Ye et. al., 2004). Yet, the number of publications on Hefei was still very limited. Lin is one of the very few scholars who have published on urban development of Hefei in English (Lin, 2009).

The selection of the survey site was done in two rounds. The first round was based on satellite image reading when a group of 3–4 villages were picked up for field visits. They were selected according to two criteria: within a reasonable distance to the ring roads (indicating the relatively new status of development, and practically with easy access), and with observable village morphology. After a few months' preparation, I visited the two cities in March 2009 to check the feasibility of doing surveys. The survey sites were decided as LJY-SJL in Xuhui District of Shanghai and the Jiadayin (贾大郢. Below as JDY) *chengzhongcun* in Baohe District of Hefei respectively (Figs. 4.4 and 4.5. Note that these images are more recent and do not reflect the situation in 2009).

Survey Protocol

The fieldwork was conditioned by the informality and high mobility of the residents in the *chengzhongcuns*. There were, however, few reliable social institutions except for the grass root government and the outpost of the public security bureau (aka. the police). Popular surveying methodologies, such as postal survey, are difficult to implement in such environment. Although most of the houses in the villages I visited did have mail boxes and regular post and/or dairy services, the post was not a reliable channel. First of all, only a few of the mail boxes seemed to be in regular use while a lot of them were in decadence. Secondly, it was difficult to find postboxes around the villages to return the completed questionnaires. Thirdly, without much preparatory knowledge or experience of survey, some of the *chengzhongcun* residents, especially those who were illiterate, would not be able to properly understand the questionnaire, let alone fill in it. Last but not the least, given the population density, it was far from uncommon to find several households cohabiting in one building. That may distort the picture, particularly regarding *per capita* housing area.

For the same reasons, it was also impractical to follow the stepwise "distribute and collect" method. In practice, I adopted a "first come first serve" strategy, i.e. take the survey into the community and try to convince every qualified people met there to fill in the questionnaire right on the spot. The only two criteria for qualifying are (1) acknowledging being a resident of the respective *chengzhongcun*, and (2) being at or above sixteen-year-old, i.e. the age to have completed secondary education and to legally enter the labor market in China.

Fig. 4.4 Location of LJN-SJL *chengzhongcuns* in Shanghai (*Source* https://map.tianditu.gov.cn/, accessed August 25, 2021)

Fig. 4.5 Location of JDY *chengzhongcun* in Hefei (*Source* https://map.tianditu.gov.cn/, accessed August 25, 2021)

Fig. 4.6 Lujiayan *chengzhongcun* residents filling in questionnaires (*Source* Photo taken by the author on June 27, 2009, Shanghai, China)

In carrying out the survey, I was assisted by graduate students from Fudan University in Shanghai and Hefei University of Technology in Hefei. Although the surveyee was expected to fill in the questionnaire on his or her own, the surveyors were ready to help explaining if necessary. The survey was held on June 27–28, 2009 in Shanghai (Fig. 4.6), and on July 11–12 the same year in Hefei. That is, at the shortest and practical interval.

The Questionnaire

The questionnaire (see Appendix) consists of three parts: the social-economic profile and housing conditions of *chengzhongcun* residents (Question 1 through 8), the channels and obstacles for settling down and getting integrated into the city (Question 9), and their perceptions on the city, the *chengzhongcun* and urban redevelopment (Question 10–11). The questionnaires used in the two cities are almost identical, with only a few places adapted to the local situation such as city names.

It is widely acknowledged that the dual system of population registration, i.e. *hukou*, and differentiated land ownership are the fundamental elements underpinning the current urban development in China. The architect Yushi Uehara developed a diagrams to grasp the spatiality of the *chengzhongcun* on the basis of the rural-urban dichotomy (Uehara, 2008: 54). Chan has also developed a similar model on the urban development in China (Chan et al., 2003: 387). However, does that dichotomy really reflect the perceptions of the people who live right on the edge?

In question 10 this nuanced relationship is represented with four diagrams. Diagram 1 and 4 represent the dichotomous view: model 1 sees the *chengzhongcun* as urban outposts in the rural area, whereas model 4 defines the *chengzhongcun* as rural island in the city. Diagram 2 and 3 reject the dichotomy by taking up a gradient of degrees of urbanisation. The differences between them, however, is that model 2, despite acknowledging the different levels of urbanization, insists that the *chengzhongcun* is always heterogeneous to the city, while model 3 sees the *chengzhongcun* as not much different from the surrounding urban environment. The fundamental implication of this test is the legitimacy of the rural-urban dichotomy.

QUALITY OF THE SURVEY

Representativeness

The *chengzhongcun* is a space of fluidity. It was difficult to obtain detailed population registration information in the *chengzhongcun*. On the part of the residents, many native *chengzhongcun* residents have moved out, while short term residents often would not be bothered to register themselves at the community office. It is a gray zone which allows some degree of freedom. From the perspective of the community officers, the community affair is divided between the Residents' Committee (RC) and the police station (Pinyin: jingwuzhan). It was practically impossible to get population data at the police stations in the two cities concerned. However, the RCs did help with rough estimations of the population. The Chuanchang RC of LJY-SJL estimated that there were 1600 to 1700 immigrants, while the number of natives was around 1200. The real number of the natives is

Table 4.1 Category breakdowns of survey respondents

Categories		Shanghai	Hefei	Percentage
Gender	Male	71	39	49
	Female	52	40	41
	Missing	10	11	9
Place of origin	Native	45	35	36
	Immigrant	86	49	61
	Missing	2	6	4
Citizenship	Urban *hukou*	8	28	16
	Rural *hukou*	46	52	44
	Missing	79	10	40

unknown, perhaps partly because the community was undergoing redevelopment at the time of the survey (June 2009). The high sensitivity of relocation compensations, which vary from household to household, makes the officers extremely alerted to enquiries concerning population and house ownership. In JDY *chengzhongcun* in Hefei, the estimation of native villagers is about 900–1000. There were no data about immigrants.

In total, the survey generated 223 valid questionnaires (133 in Shanghai and 90 in Hefei. See Table 4.1). However, it should be noted that this survey was not based on random sampling. Some people we met there declined to participate. The survey was done during day-time, which meant those who work outside the *chengzhongcun* at that very moment are missing from the population. Assuming that the ratio of immigrants to natives is the same in Hefei as in Shanghai, the survey had managed to reach around 5% of the whole population living in the *chengzhongcuns*.

Missing Values

Despite the efforts of surveyors, there were a lot of missing values in the data set. For instance, a lot of people didn't report their *hukou*. One of the reasons could be that the *hukou* is somewhat related to social status, therefore the participants do not want to reveal it to us. This is a topic that we will return to in the next chapter.

Consistency of Responses

Three pairs of mutually exclusive options in the set of question 11 were included with the intention to verify if the respondents were paying any attention when filling in the questionnaire. No. 5 and No. 6 reflect the propensity of seeing the *chengzhongcun* as urban and rural respectively. No. 10 and No. 11 place the leading role of urban development in the hand of the government and in the hands of the people respectively. No. 16 and No. 24 ask about the respondent's eagerness of moving out of or staying in the *chengzhongcun*. We were expecting the results of each individual pair of questions, and the last pair in particular, to be negatively correlated. As such, we had hoped that these "traps" would act as a quality control mechanism over the survey.

However, the size of the valid samples will be dramatically reduced if the above control mechanism is rigidly applied. For instance, only 85 out of 223 sample questionnaires would remain valid if the urban vs. rural options are controlled (neutral answers not included). In another word, the majority of respondents either think the *chengzhongcun* is both rural and urban at the same time, or are rather ambivalent about its nature (in case they choose neutral values). Nonetheless, the last set of "trap" questions proved to be more effective as only 40 respondents were self-conflicting in wishing to both stay at and leave the *chengzhongcun*.

There are reasons that may have lead some respondents not being able to be consistent in their answers. It could be that the respondents not fully understanding the meaning in the questions. After all, many of them are illiterate or have rather little formal education. It could also be that they do not want to fully disclose their opinion. Moreover, given the fact that quite a number of the questionnaires were filled in in the alleys, on kitchen tables, or held against a wall, etc., the surveyees might have been answering out of intuition rather than reason.

SURVEY ANALYSIS

Profiles of the Chengzhongcun Residents

Question No. 1 through No. 8 focus on the social-economic conditions of the *chengzhongcun* residents. For instance, the mean of length of stay is fourteen years, while the median is eight. However, for those who declare themselves as immigrants, 53% arrived in the last five years. One third of immigrants arrived within the last two years. It further validates the impression that the *chengzhongcun* is a highly mobile place.

Based on the data, we may draw the profile of a typical *chengzhongcun* resident. He or she (given the rather even gender distribution) is a 40 years old or so Han Chinese. Married, his or her household consists of three people. The house in which he or she is living at the moment belongs to a private owner. His or her education stopped at middle school. Despite reporting as having a long term job, in fact he or she works as a contracted labour. His or her monthly income lies in the interval between 1,000 and 2,000 RMB (160–320 US$).

The living condition is harsh. Most respondents report living in one room of about ten square meters. Considering the household size, half of them live with less than six square meter per person, and 20% of them even with less than three square meters per person. Most of them do not have independent kitchen, which means they would have to set up a cooking stove somewhere inside the room or under the portico. Given the popular answer that the kitchen and the bedroom is not the same room, it is very likely that they cook outside of the room in open air. In terms of water supply, most of them do have private water tap and are not dependent on public ones. However, private toilet is out of reach. They have to rely on public toilets at the street corner.

Two thirds of the immigrants report to be first generation migrants against 25% among the natives. In general, natives are reluctant to change their rural *hukou* into urban *hukou*. This is hardly surprising since the rural *hukou* is a guarantee to compensations should their *chengzhongcun* be targeted for redevelopment. Less than 20% of the immigrants declare they have ever changed their *hukou*. Interestingly, three native villagers declared that they had rather rare reverse *hukou* change from a urban *hukou* to a rural one.

The data have been submitted to statistical tests to probe the differences between the three main divisions of the respondents: location (Shanghai vs. Hefei), *hukou* (Urban vs. Rural), and place of origin (native vs. immigrants).

In general, *chengzhongcun* residents in Shanghai are younger than those in Hefei, yet they have less room to house more people (Table 4.2). Native villagers have been in the *chengzhongcun* for a longer period than the immigrants, and have more rooms and large rooms. They are even younger than the immigrants. Urban people tend to stay longer and have more rooms.

Table 4.2 One-Way ANOVA Analysis of interval socio-economic data

	Age	Length of stay (year)	Number of rooms	Room size (Sq. M.)	Number of resident
Shanghai vs. Hefei	+			+	+
Native vs. Immigrant	+	+	+	+	
Urban vs. Rural		+	+		
a. + significant at α = 0.05					

Pearson Chi-Square Analysis (Table 4.3) further reveals some of the differences across the divisions. In Shanghai most of the houses are owned by native villagers and leased out to immigrants, whereas in Hefei immigrants also own a considerable amount of houses in which they settled their own family rather than leasing out. In Shanghai, most of the people have to depend on public water supply. By comparison, the majority of *chengzhongcun* residents in Hefei have private access to tap water. Even more severe is the toilet supply in Shanghai, only 9 people out of 133 respondents report that they have a private toilet. In Hefei, the majority have their own toilet, even though less than half of them depend on public toilet. In terms of employment, most of the people in Shanghai are able to find a category that suits their employment, whereas in Hefei a sizable part of the respondents associate themselves with "Others" as employment.

The natives are better off than immigrants in "Use right", "Kitchen", "Tap water", "Toilet", and "Employment". Comparing urban and rural population, the former is at a better position in "Use right", "Kitchen", "Toilet".

For ordinal data in question 1.4 and 8.3, a Kruskal Wallis Test is applied (Table 4.4). Only entries with significant differences are listed in the table. The level of "Education" favours the natives. Those living in Shanghai have a higher "Income" than in Hefei.

Channels and Obstacles Toward Urban Integration

Chengzhongcun residents are eye witnesses of the contrast between urban and rural China. The very fact that some of them emigrated from rural

Table 4.3 Pearson Chi-Square Analysis of categorical socio-economic data

	Gender	Ethnicity	Marriage	Ownership	Use right	Kitchen	Bedroom	Tap water	Toilet	Employment	Job type
Shanghai vs. Hefei				+	+			+	+	+	
Native vs. Immigrant					+	+		+	+	+	
Urban vs. Rural					+	+			+		

a. + significant at $\alpha = 0.05$

Table 4.4 Kruskal Wallis Test of ordinal socio-economic data

Native vs. Immigrant	
	Education
Chi-Square	4,965
Df	1
Asymp. Sig	,026
Shanghai vs. Hefei	
	Income
Chi-Square	16,366
Df	1
Asymp. Sig	,000

Table 4.5 Correspondence Analysis of obstacles to urban integration

Summary

Dimension					*Proportion of inertia*		*Confidence singular value*	
								Correlation
	Singular value	*Inertia*	*Chi Square*	*Sig.*	*Accounted for*	*Cumulative*	*Standard deviation*	*2*
1	0.475	0.225			0.730	0.730	0.063	0.074
2	0.264	0.069			0.225	0.954	0.078	
3	0.119	0.014			0.046	1.000		
Total		0.309	42.001	0.001ᵃ	1.000	1.000		
ᵃ18 degrees of freedom								

areas to the city explained their preference. Notwithstanding the seem-ingly brighter future, the process of urbanisation is not an easy one. Question 9 gives two sets of seven options on the potential channels and obstacles to integration in the city from which the *chengzhongcun* resi-dents were suggested to pick out three and list them in a descending order. The most popular combination for set one is "Finding a job", "Admission to higher education" and "Purchasing a house" and for set two "Income level", "Education level" and "*Hukou*".

Correspondence Analysis is applied to gauge the relationship between the seven options and four different sets of combinations of location and origin (Table 4.5 and Fig. 4.7). Dimension 1, to which immigrants in

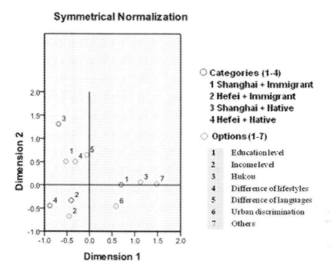

Fig. 4.7 Correspondence Analysis of obstacles toward urban integration

both Shanghai and Hefei associate, accounts for more than 70% of the variance. The natives of Shanghai lie far from other categories. In the meantime, people in Hefei, whether native or immigrants, identify with the obstacle of "Income level". It could be explained by the relatively low income in Hefei compared to Shanghai. To immigrants in Shanghai, the "*hukou*" and "Urban discrimination" consist of the most significant obstacle towards urbanisation. "Education", "Difference of lifestyles" and "Difference of languages" (dialects), are not really relevant.

In order to obtain a compounded ranking, Principle Component Analysis (PCA) is applied. The frequency of each the seven options that lies in different combinations of location and origin is then multiplied with their respective score (assuming first rank weights 3, second rank weights 2, and the third 1). For question 9.1, i.e. the channels toward urbanization, the analysis give only one principal component (PC), which is rather evenly distributed among the seven options. The final ranking is 1325476. In other words, "Long term employment", "Purchasing a house" and "Admission to higher education" are the most important means to achieve urban identity. "Join the army", which once used to be preferred by rural youth, has lost its appeal nowadays.

Table 4.6 Rotated Component Matrix (Varimax) on obstacles to urban integration

	Component 1	2
Education level	,894	,026
Income level	,818	,380
Hukou	,924	,335
Difference of lifestyles	,525	,157
Difference of languages	,106	,954
Urban discrimination	,961	,260
Others	,391	,876

Extraction Method: Principal Component Analysis
Rotation Method: Varimax with Kaiser Normalization
a. Rotation converged in 3 iterations

For question 9.2, i.e. the obstacles toward urbanization, there are two principle components (Table 4.6). PC 1 (accounts for 65% cumulative variance) has high loadings on option 6, 3, 1 and 2, and PC 2 has high loadings on option 5 and 7. It could be said that PC 1 is institutional oriented, and PC 2 is personal oriented. For PC 1, the compounded ranking is 2316475. The most important obstacles toward urbanization are "Income level", "*Hukou*", and "Education level". For PC 2, the ranking is 2357641. Interestingly, in both cases the most important two are identical, while option 4 "Difference of lifestyles" is not important at all in both cases. It seems that to the *chengzhongcun* inhabitants, lifestyle differences is not something that could trouble them.

To conclude, stable employment and purchasing power on the housing market are the most important elements in the urban integration process, while the *hukou* system and income level are the most difficult barriers faced by *chengzhongcun* residents. It may be inferred that their dream of the city is very much restrained by their human capital. Even if the purchasing power could be raised via improved employment, there is still the last obstacle to be overcome: the *hukou*.

PERCEPTIONS OF THE *CHENGZHONGCUN* RESIDENTS

Question 10 tested model recognition of the rural-urban relationship. As mentioned before, the dual system of land ownership and population registration are by and large complement with each other. Therefore, the

spatial diagram could also be interpreted as reflecting the social configuration, i.e. the division of the population into urban and rural *hukou*
holders. 61% of the population has chosen the second model, i.e. the
chengzhongcun as a heterogeneous space within a gradient of urban-rural
continuum. It shows, on the one hand, the people of the *chengzhongcun*
are highly aware of the differences between their community and the city;
on the other, they reject the black and white divide of the urban and the
rural spaces, as 79% chose for one of the gradient models. In social sense,
it may be read as they reject the dichotomy of *hukou* status that overly
simplified the social conditions. Only 9% of the residents selected the
diagram that would confirm the social and spatial urban/rural divide, i.e.
the fourth one. In other words, the *hukou* system has lost its legitimacy.

Chi-Square Analysis between the choice of models and the differenti-
ating categories (*hukou*, place of origin, and city) shows that the choice of
diagrams vary significantly when sorted by *hukou* ($P = 0.037$). Diagram
No.2 has the highest popularity among rural people. In other words,
compared to urban people, the rural people are highly aware of the differences between the village and the city outside. At the same time, they
reject the idea that, between urban and rural, there is a clear cut divide.
This is understandable because they are the victims of the rural-urban
dichotomy, and the contrast between the village and the city is more
striking to them than to natives or urbanites.

Question 11 is a set of 25 questions aiming to evaluate the opinions
of the respondents on the *chengzhongcun*, their life in it, and their view
on the general urbanisation process. The questions were designed in clus-
ters but positioned randomly in the questionnaire. To each question, the
respondent is expected to give a score between 1 and 5 with 5 meaning
"Strongly pro" and 1 the opposite.

All the questions have a positive above-average response, except the
questions 11.5, 11.8, 11.18, 11.19 and 11.22, for which the means is
less than 3, i.e. the responses tend to be negative. A closer look on the
respective questions reveals part of the reason: 11.8 ("I live here because I
can't get integrated in the city"), 11.18 ("I didn't benefit from urbanisation") and 11.22 ("The *chengzhongcun* lacks a sense of neighbourhood")
are all negative. Therefore, these responses actually confirm to the positive attitude of the respondents. Question 11.5 and 11.19, on the other
hand, are positive statements. In this case, the responses to these two
questions are indeed rejecting the given statements. Put it simply, the
general population do not think "the *chengzhongcun* is urban", and they

do not think the redevelopment of the *chengzhongcun* would "destroy their community". While the first one is hardly surprising, the second is an interesting point of view: it seems to show that the sense of community is not bounded to the physical space. It is more likely that they organize their community along the line of *hukou*, place of origin, kinship, etc. Put it in another way, no matter for the natives or the immigrants, their community has little to do with the *chengzhongcun* itself.

We also submit Question 11 to a Kruskal Wallis Test using the same three division lines (Shanghai/Hefei, Immigrant/Native, and Urban/Rural) (Table 4.7). Only entries with significant differences are listed in the table.

It shows that native people appear to favour urban redevelopment to be "Led by the Government". Immigrants, on the other hand, tend to respond that they "Would like to stay", and would like to "Change their *hukou*" (mostly from rural to urban).

The rural population also reports more that they "Would like to stay" in the *chengzhongcun*. At the meantime, they also report higher level of un-satisfaction about the distribution of benefits in urban redevelopment.

Table 4.7 Kruskal Wallis Test on opinions of the respondents

Native vs. Immigrant

	Urbanization led by the government	Want to change *hukou*	Would stay
Chi-Square	3,876	4,042	4,207
Df	1	1	1
Asymp. Sig	,049	,044	,040

Urban vs. Rural

	Didn't benefit from urbanisation	Would stay	
Chi-Square	4,289	8,069	
Df	1	1	
Asymp. Sig	0,038	0,005	

Shanghai vs. Hefei

	Used to the urban lifestyle	Redevelopment benefits me	Over-crowded
Chi-Square	13,544	6,498	6,103
Df	1	1	1
Asymp. Sig	0,000	0,011	0,013

Not surprisingly, people in Shanghai report a higher level of adaptation to the "Urban lifestyle" than in Hefei. They are also more sensitive to the "Over-crowdedness" of the *chengzhongcun*. But when it comes to redevelopment of the *chengzhongcun*, people in Hefei are more confident that they could benefit from it.

In order to probe the determining factor(s) of *chengzhongcun* residents' evaluations, Logistic Regression is applied. Responses that are not binomial had been transformed into binomial data by taking the neutral answer as the threshold. For Question 11, the entries were transformed by taking the values equal to or lower than 3 as null, and those above 3 as one (answers to the negative questions were reversed to ensure they were positively ordered). For all the 25 questions, those with significant results are summarized below (Table 4.8).

Take question 11.24 as an example. It is significantly and positively associated with the "Length of stay". It means that the longer a resident reports to have stayed in the *chengzhongcun*, the higher chance that he or she would also report willingness to stay there. Indeed, the results (not included here) prove "Length of stay" to be the most important explanatory factor in the opinions of the respondents.

The level of education correlates positively with the view on the effect of the 2010 Shanghai EXPO (in Hefei, the corresponding option is the Grand Construction (Pinyin: da jianshe) movement, see Chapter 5). On the other hand, the positive correlation between marriage and the desire to change *hukou* could perhaps be explained by the fact that married people feel more constraints living in a city without the local urban *hukou*. Without it, many essential social rights, such as medical care and children education, etc. are out of the reach of the family. This is an issue that will be returned to in the next chapter.

CONCLUSION

In this chapter I have tried to probe the *chengzhongcun* residents' view on various issues in and beyond their community. The *chengzhongcun* is a very diverse community, where people have different living conditions as well as different viewpoints. The results from this survey tell a different *chengzhongcun* from the stereotype of a dull, passive and desperate community. On the contrary, it is vibrant and dynamic, full of people moving to take the advantage of this rural niche in the urban world. In this sense, it is really a zone of contact and transformation.

Table 4.8 Summary of logistic regressions on *chengzhongcun* residents' opinion

	Age	Sex	Marriage	Education	Stay	Native/Immigrant	Urban/Rural	Income	Constant
11.1 *Chengzhongcun* city different							−		
11.3 More urban, higher living std				−					
11.4 More urban, more happiness	+								
11.5 *Chengzhongcun* is urban					−				
11.7 Redevelopment benefits me							+		
11.13 Want to change Hukou			+						
11.15 Forced to relocate									+
11.17 Rural life better than city life		+							
11.18 I didn't benefit from urbanization							−		
11.21 EXPO is good to the city				+					
11.22 *Chengzhongcun* lacks community					−				
11.23 The people is underrepresented	+								
11.24 Would like to stay here					+				

	Age	Sex	Marriage	Education	Stay	Native/Immigrant	Urban/Rural	Income	Constant
11.25 *Chengzhongcun* is more livable					+				

a. +positive coefficient ($\alpha = 0.05$)
b. −negative coefficient ($\alpha = 0.05$)

Indeed, many report that the *chengzhongcun* is at the very same time an urban and rural place, a curious view that long predates scholarly terminology such as *cheng*-cum-*xiang* (Tang, 2019).

However, to romanticize the *chengzhongcun* is anything but the aim of this study. No doubt that the *chengzhongcun* was and still is the space for the marginalization. In spite of the great resilience of the *chengzhongcun* residents, their chance of upgrading into the urban world is still impeded by several constraints. Income and education are among the most important ones, but they are still secondary to *hukou*, the Chinese domestic citizenship system. For most of the *chengzhongcun* residents, it is beyond their reach to change their *hukou* status. Even though the urban-rural dichotomy has lost its legitimacy, people are still being categorized as rural or urban citizens.

Looking back from the standing point in 2021, it was only in later years that similar case studies on the basis of surveys were carried out in Shenzhen (Tao et. al., 2014) and Wenzhou (Lin & Li, 2017). These surveys were tuned to focusing on the residential satisfaction of rural migrants, some of whom lived in the urban villages, aka. *chengzhongcuns*. However, by putting the word "satisfaction" into survey is problematic in itself because this act conveys an intrinsic positive attitude.

Are rural migrants in Chinese cities satisfied with the status quo? Do *chengzhongcun* residents feel happy? It depends on how they understand and enact happiness. But to suggest that they are mere passive subjects of the *hukou* system is also misleading. While they suffer from the artificial and obsolete policy, the struggle of citizenship rights has never stopped. In the next chapter, I will showcase a project utilizing creativity in the fight for citizenship rights.

References

Chan, K. W. (2007). Misconceptions and complexities in the study of China's cities: Definitions, statistics, and implications. *Euroasian Geography and Economics, 48*(4), 383–412. https://doi.org/10.2747/1538-7216.48.4.383

Chan, R. C. K., Yao, Y. M., & Zhao, S. X. B. (2003). Self-help housing strategy for temporary population in Guangzhou, China. *Habitat International, 27*(1), 19–35. https://doi.org/10.1016/S0197-3975(02)00033-4

Chung, H. (2010). Building an image of villages-in-the-city: A clarification of China's distinct urban spaces. *International Journal of Urban and Regional*

Research, 34(2), 421–437. https://doi.org/10.1111/j.1468-2427.2010.009
79.x

Gamble, S. D. (2011). Peking: A social survey. Brill.

Gregor, K. (2008). Mixed use, mixed emotions. The Austin Chronicle, available at: http://www.austinchronicle.com/news/2008-02-01/586589/ [accessed November 21, 2011].

Lan, Y. Y. (2004). Villages in the metropolis: Field studies on a new village community [Pinyin: dushi li de cunzhuang: yige xin cunshe gongtongti de shidi yanjiu]. SDX Joint Publishing Company.

Lin, G. C. S. (2009). Developing China: Land, politics and social conditions. Routledge.

Lin, S. N., & Li, Z. G. (2017). Residential satisfaction of migrants in Wenzhou, an 'ordinary city' of China. Habitat International, 66, 76–85. https://doi.org/10.1016/j.habitatint.2017.05.004

Lu, H. (1995). Creating urban outcasts: Shantytowns in Shanghai, 1920–1950. Journal of Urban History, 21(5), 563–596. https://doi.org/10.1177/009614429502100501

Minhang District Archive, Shanghai Municipality. (1953). Documents related to demolition of shanty towns along the Suzhou Creek. Catalogue number: MHDA51-2-587 1953 [accessed July 3, 2010].

Minhang District Archive, Shanghai Municipality. (1956). Statistic report on agricultural land use acreage of Xijiao district in 1956. Catalogue number: MHDA57-2-100 1956 [accessed July 3 2010].

Minhang District Archive, Shanghai Municipality. (1958). Report to the district committee [of Xijiao district] on the allocation of peasants from Xuhui district etc., whose land has been expropriated. Catalogue number: MHDA57-2-204 1958. [accessed July 3, 2010].

Tang, W. S. (2019). Town-country relations in China: Back to basics. Eurasian Geography and Economics, 60(4), 455–485. https://doi.org/10.1080/15387216.2019.1686407

Tao, L., Wong, F. K. W., & Hui, E. C. M. (2014). Residential satisfaction of migrant workers in China: A case study of shenzhen. Habitat International, 42, 193–202. https://doi.org/0.1016/j.habitatint.2013.12.006

Uehara, Y. (2008). Unknown urbanity: Towards the village in the city. In L. Liauw (Ed.), "New Urban China", a special issue of the Architectural Design, 78(5), 52–55. https://doi.org/10.1002/ad.738

Vaughn, E. (2006). Sadness at inevitable changes. The Austin Chronicle, available at: http://www.austinchronicle.com/postmarks/2006-10-09/409427/ [accessed November 21, 2011].

Ye, P. (2005). Survey and analysis on the "village in city" problem in Hefei. Masters' Thesis, College of Architecture & Art, Hefei University of Technology [in Chinese].

Ye, P., & Xu, X. (2008). Measures for harmonious remodeling of the "village-in-city" in Hefei. *Journal of Hefei University of Technology, 31*(11), 1867–1871 [in Chinese].

Ye, P., Xu, X., & Wang, L. (2004). First exploration of the remodeling of the "village in city" in Hefei. *Architectural Journal, 11*, 23–26 [in Chinese].

Zheng, S. Q., Long, F. J., Fan, C. C., & Gu, Y. Z. (2009). Urban villages in China: A 2008 survey of migrant settlements in Beijing. *Eurasian Geography and Economics, 50*(4), 425–446. https://doi.org/10.2747/1539-7216.50.4.425

CHAPTER 5

Resistance, Public Art and Citizenship

Abstract In this chapter a case of using public art in the protest for citizenship in a *chengzhongcun* community is documented. Drawing upon the new literature on citizenship studies, public art, and participatory governance, the organization process and contents and strategy of this event are analyzed. The Chinese citizenship as embodied in the hukou system predetermines the access to basic social rights, such as housing and education. Rural immigrants and their children in the city are excluded from enjoying these rights. Against that milieu, the "Happiness Hefei" project raised the question of happiness at a time when Chinese cities are enjoying unprecedented prosperity. A provocative strategy of bringing art into the *chengzhongcun* was adopted. While the art exhbition is far from a straightforward criticism, it succeeded in creating an interruption to the lives and notions of ordinary urban middle class. Public art, as demonstrated in this case, constitutes an agent and object of a public pedagogy of citizenship rights.

Keywords Public art · Citizenship · Biennale · Hefei · Carnivalesque

> *Whereas in the West we are witnessing the breaking of society, in China, the society has still to be produced.* (Kuah-Pearce and Guiheux, 2009, p. 17)

INTRODUCTION

In recent years there is a resurgence of studies on the Chinese citizenship (Li et al., 2010; Zhang, 2010a), which revives the preceding researches in the 1990s (Solinger, 1995, 1999). Compared to the rich literature on the history, process and condition of urban China, critical reflections on citizenship-centered struggle are in dearth. Not to be mistaken is that some researches on urban grassroots movements do deal with struggles on property rights or political rights (see for example Gui et al., 2009). However, the problem is that they assume a common citizenship to city residents, which is not true. The Chinese citizenship, as embodied in the *hukou* system, is characterized with its rural–urban binary. Those living in the city without urban citizenship, i.e. immigrants, are largely dropped out of the picture of citizenship struggles. We know little, for instance, how the rural immigrants practice their citizenship in the city. And if there is any struggle for citizenship rights by the immigrants, who is involved in and what kind of strategy has been adopted?

The shortage of studies on citizenship struggles by the immigrants is understandable. Citizenship has always been a political issue which is inherently exclusive by nature. In the case of China, the rights of the rural population in general, and rural immigrants in the city in specific, are less privileged in this policy design. Despite recurrent debates on abolition of the discriminative *hukou* System, as a national policy it persisted to date. There is little motivation for a top-down reform, since "no entity within the state - and no party in opposition, for, of course, there were none in China at this time - would be motivated to seek their (i.e. rural immigrants) support" (Solinger, 1999). On the other hand, a bottom-up revolution of citizenship is problematic if not inconceivable. The struggle for citizenship rights of rural immigrants in Chinese cities requires a new approach.

In this paper I will introduce a case of using public art in the protest for citizenship in a deprived urban community. The so-called "Happiness Hefei: the Second Contemporary Art Biennale" took place partly in a village north to the city of Hefei in eastern China on May 8–9, 2010. The exhibition invites audiences from all the social strata to a village of native and immigrant peasants. Under the theme of happiness, the audiences were encouraged to interact with artists and with each other. This exhibition is extraordinary in the sense that it was the first art event to be held in a deprived *chengzhongcun* in the city. In so doing, it succeeded in evoking a broad public attention on the local situation. Partly due to this act, the immigrant children's right to formal urban education was eventually realized.

Drawing upon the new literature on citizenship studies (Isin & Turner, 2007; Lawy & Biesta, 2006), public art (Pinder, 2008; White, 2008), and participatory governance (Gaventa, 2004), I will review the organization process and analyze the contents and strategy of this event. Firstly, I will confront citizenship in general and Chinese citizenship in specific by positioning it into the new developments of citizenship studies. Then I will examine the emerging strategy of using public art in citizenship struggles. Thereafter, details of the "Happiness Hefei: the Second Hefei Contemporary Art Biennale" will be assembled so as to reconstruct the whole process. Based on comparative readings of literature of citizenship pedagogy and public art, as well as relevant reportages, notes of the curators and comments from the audiences, the underpinning dynamics of this art exhibition will be revealed.

CITIZENSHIP DECONSTRUCTED

The Right to Education Under the Hukou *System*

Despite the improvisation in recent researches, the core issue of citizenship in the Chinese context is always the *hukou* system. Initially setup for the purpose of population registration at the beginning of the Socialist era, however, in practice *hukou* acts as an institutionalised tool of access control to the city and its welfare system (Cheng & Selden, 1994). Besides the managerial function, its robust economic power have lead Solinger to call it an "urban public goods regime" (Solinger, 1995), to which the rural population is largely excluded. With the introduction of economic reform in the late 1970s, the Chinese government had virtually switched to the direction of market economy. However, while the mobility control of rural to urban migration loosened in early 1980s, as a necessary step towards economy liberalization, the *hukou* system was retained. As a matter of fact, despite its Socialist root, the *hukou* system has been in effect for a much longer time after the reform than before it.

This peculiar policy design has helped to maintain the rural–urban binary. Under the framework of statehood, the Chinese citizenship is divided between the urban and the rural. There are also numerous

types of semi-citizenship or quasi-citizenship issued by local city governments throughout the country and could be acquired by market means.
Favoring those who with outstanding financial or human capital, this
policy has been criticized for facilitating developmentalism at the national
level (Chen, 2009), and urban entrepreneurship at the local level (Zhang,
2010a). On the other hand, the exclusiveness of citizenship becomes most
visible when coming into terms with immigrants. Historically, the partial
acceptance of immigrant labourers, i.e. "take the labor without confer-
ring the rights of membership" (Morris, 1994), has been a universal
phenomenon whenever and wherever large scale migration happens.
Nonetheless, there is no exaggeration of the problem in China considering the volume of the rural to urban migration is over 221 million
according to the Sixth National Population Census of China (NPCC)
in the year of 2010.

Compared to their urban compatriots, rural immigrants are at a vulnerable position with little chance to improve their status. Urban housing,
for example, is inaccessible to them during the Socialist era and more
often than not beyond their affordability after the reform. Apart from the
collective dormitories provided by the employer or make-shift shelters,
such as on construction sites, many of the immigrants have to "self help"
in finding housing (Zhang et al., 2003). Adding to the burden of self-
helping housing is the rather rigid control of Chinese cities on informal
settlements. Unlike in some other developing countries where slum mushroomed at the fringe of the city, in China there is no institutional room
for slum to grow. Consequently, it was the villages located on the urban
fringe that accommodated many of the rural immigrants when the native
peasants lease out their spare housing space for extra incomes.

Education exclusion is another aspect of the *hukou* system. In principal,
Chinese children have the right and obligation to education. However,
when put into practice it is to say that the children of immigrant workers
should attend school at their place of origin. Indeed, many of the migrant
parents have left their children back in their hometown villages. But even
disregarding the quality differences of education in the city and the countryside, the long term separation of the children from their parents has
become a big social problem. Studies have shown that the "left behind
children" (Pinyin: liushou ertong) have higher chance to suffer from
communication difficulties and even psychological problems (Liang et al.,
2008; Liu, 2009). Although, in principal, immigrants' children have been
given the right to attend urban public schools at a reduced fee since

2003, it is difficult to realize for practical reasons such as affordability and employment mobility of their parents. Therefore, the children are effectively "denied them even the most fundamental tools just for 'set[ting] the state' for a entry into the polity" (Solinger, 1999).

Other exclusive aspects of the urban *hukou* such as medical care, pension or employment protection, etc., have posed a striking contradiction to the norm of classical citizenship. Interestingly, as a point of reference, many of the aforementioned studies vest their arguments on the creed of Thomas H. Marshall (Li et al., 2010; Solinger, 1999). Since the welfare state regime had gained popularity in the Post-war years, this rendering of citizenship has resulted in the "nationalization of citizenship" (Isin & Turner, 2007), in which the citizenship and the nationality have become synonyms. Marshall is known for having proclaimed that "citizenship is a status bestowed on all those who are full members of a community" (Marshall, 1950). In other words, the fact of holding the nationality of a given state means the bearer has citizenship rights and vice versa. This view of citizenship, however, has little to do China since it has never been a welfare state. The urban *hukou* system of the Socialist era resembles to the welfare state citizenship in some ways, but in practice the rights of citizenship are unequally distributed, particularly after the reform when cities are given more autonomy in making their own bylaws.

Citizenship Mobilized

Another problem of referring to Marshall is the neglect of new developments in citizenship studies. Marshal's vision of the citizenship is certainly at its mature stage. However, his optimism has underestimated "the continuing dependence of citizenship on the economic growth and the important role played by struggles to establish citizenship rights as well as the need for continued struggles to maintain them" (Heisler, 1991, p. 459). While it had characterized the Post-war welfare state regimes, recent critiques have pointed out Marshall's failure to take into account the backlash of the market and the state that would act in a biased way. On the ground, citizenship is constantly subject to social conditions, such as regional differences, ethnical, religious, and racial issues. For instance, various versions of affirmative acts testify to the complicated process of integration and assimilation of foreign immigrants or even nationals of the same country. There is also a concern about citizenship education for young people through initiatives of "practicing citizenship" (Lowy and Biesta, 2006), so that they can acquire the full citizenship and understand the duties and rights. Hardly surprising, at a higher level, transnational cosmopolitan citizenship built upon the consensus that "we are all part of humanity is often the premise, but it is a premise whose idealism greatly exceeds its substance" (Beauregard and Bounds 2000). To secure and realize citizenship requires much more than an idealized norm. Citizenship is not necessarily static or homogeneous, but rather should be taken as "practiced rather than a given" (Gaventa, 2004).

By making a seemingly static notion dynamic, the question is how to enact the citizenship. As Engin Isin has explained, "if act is understood against habitus, practice, conduct, discipline and routine (the latter conceived of as ordered and ordering qualities of how humans conduct themselves), we can then perhaps understand why the question of acts would remain minor and fragmented within social and political thought and the social sciences" (Isin, 2009, p. 379). After all, citizenship could be meaningful only if applied in either positive or negative way. That is to say, to act according to the duty of citizenship, and to fight for the rights that the citizenship entails. In deprived urban communities such as *chengzhongcun*, the struggle is a daily matter rather than a once and for all bid. By this token, the strategy of resistance should also adapt to the fact that the immigrants either have little awareness of it or are in lack of sufficient social capital to organize a protest. The act of citizenship calls for a new type of public space whereby formal or informal negotiation is possible.

PUBLIC ART AND CITIZENSHIP PEDAGOGY

Public art is believed to have "the potential to provide a stage for the active exercise of citizenship roles" (Reiter, 2009, p. 158). This potential is deeply rooted in the three-fold relationship between art and citizenship. Firstly, practicing art is, among others, a creative way to achieve citizenship rights (White, 2008). Then, art affects the learning process of citizenship and hence helps to redefining the later as a dynamic instead of static matter (Biesta, 2006). Thirdly, citizenship rights include the rights to art, without which the citizenship is incomplete (Holton, 2000). Put it in other words, access to art is a right granted by the citizenship and conversely the citizenship could also be partly defined with the constituent of art. Therefore, enacting art is also a means to enact citizenship. Public art is practiced, disseminated, and interpreted through a democratic process on which the classical citizenship is constructed.

It's worth noting that the use of public art in the city is anything but new. The aesthetic nature of art has traditionally been exploited to beautify urban spaces such as buildings' facade or squares. Modern incarnations of this tradition can still be felt in urban regeneration projects (Sharp et al., 2005). However, the critical aspect of public art was not discovered until as late as in the 1990s. Pinder has linked art with politics and pedagogy by deeming them all as forms of urban intervention (Pinder, 2008). A further observation confirms that public art soundly corresponds to the three critiques of public pedagogy (Biesta, 2012), that is: for the public, of the public, and enabling the public-ness. In a rather anonymous sphere such as in the field of public art, no one is at a prioritized position of instructing. Rather, art is a preferable cause to bring people together and hence facilitate public engagements through artistic actions. Moreover, public art can be eruptive to norms such as the stereotype of impoverished areas equal to cultural desert (Pinyin: wenhua shamo). Quite on the contrary, public art poses a huge "interruption" to habitual norms when it takes grip in the otherwise stigmatized deprived communities.

In comparison with other forms of citizenship struggles, public art has the unbeaten advantage of profoundness, subtlety, and flexibility. Art can be exaggerating, satirical or metaphorical, but it can also be realistic and straightforward. Applying art instead of violence, the excluded "other" is heard, seen, and sometimes touched. Public art empowers the marginalized people and helps them to reclaim the rights entitled by their citizenship, which used to be only partially exercised. Short-lasted though, the ephemeral nature (Minty, 2006; White, 2008) of public art actions are good at creating what might be called "carnivalesque" (White, 2008, p. 39) atmosphere, which would induce long term changes. On this point, public art not only rejects the singular perspective of citizenship based on commonalities, but also politically connects the public pedagogy with act of citizenship.

There have been quite some successful cases of using artistic means in acts of citizenship worldwide. Before and after the apartheid in South Africa, public art encouraged to act as a transcending agency of memorizing, protesting, and eventually healing the social scar (Minty, 2006). Two crucial changes have facilitated the use of art: the "transformation of existing institutions" and the expansion of "financing pool" in the market. Similarly, a *favela* drum school setup by famous musician in the city of Salvador, Brazil, has achieved a huge success in fighting segregation (Reiter, 2009). It not only provides the music loving *favela* youth a place of performance, but also attracts outsiders into the *favela*. Thanks to this initiative, that community eventually gets integrated into the city and is no longer a *favela*. Moreover, the Mourinho Project (*Projeto Morrinho*) has stirred wide attention on *favela* by bringing out, rather than get people in, the *favela* to be displayed at public places around the world. Cases from developed countries such as Canada and the UK also add to the experience of citizenship practices (Grundy & Boudreau, 2008; Lawy et al.,. 2010).

In the next sections I will introduce and analyze an art exhibition organized to be displayed in *chengzhongcun*. It will provide us a special case of citizenship struggles in the Chinese context.

STAGING ART INTO A *CHENGZHONGCUN*

Urban Development in Hefei

Located at over 400 km from the eastern coast of China, the layout of the city of Hefei remained but a medium-sized provincial city until the late 1990s. Thereafter, urban construction took off in Hefei by following the models of coastal cities to set up "Economic Development Zones" (EDZs). New zones were carved out from suburban districts or subordinate counties and then converted into urban districts (Lin, 2009). The first decade of this century witnessed a new tide of urban expansion when the city government opted for a more aggressive strategy as crystallized in the official motto "Grand Construction" (Pinyin: da jianshe). According to the Hefei City Comprehensive Plan 2006–2020, by 2010 the built-up urban area shall be 300 square kilometers, and by 2020 that will be 360 square kilometers. Not surprisingly, despite the "urban" tag, many places of the newly established districts are yet to be urbanised. There is a mixture in the landscape where rural and urban fabrics coexist. Villages have been accommodating rural immigrants since the 1990s. Depends on the scope and criteria, the volume of *chengzhongcun* in Hefei varies from 75 (Ye & Xu, 2008, data of 2006) to 358 (Li, 2008, data of 2008).

Informal Education, Migrant Children and Civil Society

Huangqiao village is located in the northern suburb of Hefei. Like many of its peers, it is a typical *chengzhongcun* (Fig. 5.1). But Huangqiao is different because it is not only the home to hundreds of residents but also to a school. The Huangqiao Immigrants' Children Primary School provides pre-school and elementary level education to immigrants' children in Huangqiao and neighboring villages. It has in total 111 elementary level students and 12 pre-school children. In terms of budget, the students pay around 400–500 RMB (roughly equals to 70–80 US$) every semester, while the nine teaching staff receive a nominal salary of 600–700 RMB per month (as a reference, the minimum salary of Hefei city was 720 RMB per month as of 2010, which was raised to 1010 RMB in May 2011) for their part time teaching job. The school, however, is not recognised by the educational authority of Luyang district, Hefei municipality. As a result, it receives no public funding from the government and has to rely on donations to keep operating.

This illegal but effective *in-situ* solution was made possible partly due to the acquiescence of the authority, and partly due to the efforts of philanthropic activists including writers, businessmen, journalists, civil servants, and university students. These people are, roughly speaking, from a background of the urban middle class. Mr. Xu Duoyu, a writer, has been both donating directly and inviting donations from outside using his contacts. As a matter of fact, thanks to this social network, it was during one of the donate trips to the Huangqiao school in January 2010 that

Fig. 5.1 Huangqiao village (left) seen from above the viaduct bridge (right) (*Source* photographs taken by the author, Jul. 14, 2010, Hefei, China)

two artists Mr. Zhang Yuanping and Mr. Huang Zhen came up with the idea to host the Hefei Biennial in Huangqiao.

Under the theme of "Happiness Hefei", the biennale consists of four sessions, namely the "Happiness is Itch-scratching" performance on Huaihe Rd. Pedestrian Shopping Street on April 18; the "Huangqiao Happiness Project" on May 8–9; a comprehensive exhibition in the Kurume Art Museum during June 5–14, and new media seminars in the Digital Arts Centre at the University of Science & Technology of China during June 15–21. The Huangqiao exhibition was displayed inside village and under a viaduct bridge to the East. Apart from the display of "conventional" art works, such as oil and digital painting, photograph and sculpture, avant-garde arts including installations and performance arts were given priority. More than 70 artists took part in the "Huangqiao Happiness Project" individually or in group. A few dozens of national and local media covered this exhibition.

No wonder that the Huangqiao session was the most attended of the four, and no less the most controversial. Since it was publicized mainly via online forums, it had reached a wide audience from the local internet users many of who attended the exhibition. All though there was no statistic of the audiences since it was displayed in half-open space and no entrance control was implemented, various resources estimated that between 3,000 and 4,000 people came to Huangqiao on the first day (Anonymous, 2010). On December 10 2010, an archive compilation of texts and photographs of the biennale was published and released during a salon meeting by the organizers on the topic of "In search of the citizen".

DIAGNOSING HAPPINESS IN A *CHENGZHONGCUN*

Urban Resistance and the Engaging Art

In recently years, the wellbeing of the people has gained more attention in popular media as well as in official reports. As a background, the economic development in China has resulted in an enlarged gap between the groups who have benefited from it and those have not. Little has been changed on the scale and degree of exploitation of the rural immigrants which has lead scholar to envisage civil protests long time ago (Solinger, 1995, 1999). But the experience of civil struggle shows that even if the struggle is collectively organized, such as in factories of the industrialized coastal area, external assistance in legal and organizational terms are still needed (Froissart, 2009). Individual or small scale resistance is, sadly, constantly overshadowed by the repressive urban governance. The fear of violent crackdown has always been a part of the psychology of urban protest (Kuah-Pearce & Guiheux, 2009). It is against this background that the question of "happiness" is raised in Hefei.

Art critics have observed how the subversive nature of modern art has worked in the context of China (Sullivan, 1999; Wiseman, 2007). The enthusiasm of social concern in art was transformed into Cynical Realism after the dramatic turn in 1989 (Berghuis, 2006; Sullivan, 1999). Characterized by its exposure of confusion and absurdity, performance art is especially controversial since the social reality the artists are engaging with is predominately based on the power framework that they are about to criticize. In light of this, Wiseman and Berghuis both recognize the importance of "open engagement" with the society, even if the same society has made artists to "work at a level below that of discourse, at the level of matter" (Wiseman, 2007, p. 119). The presence of art and artists are meaningful enough if further interpretation is limited. After all, it is beyond the power of the artists to address the citizenship question or social justice fundamentally.

The engaging stance was clear ever since the initial stage the Hefei Biennale. The choice of a *chengzhongcun* for an art exhibition was not coincidental. Zhang, one of the two curators, said in an interview, "During our visit to the primary school, we saw the clash between the city and the countryside in a dramatic transformation of Chinese economy, and we came up with the concept of 'Huangqiao Happiness Project'" (Feng et. al., 2010). The other curator Liu also said, "Actually we also have some minor 'goals'. Compared to the fast growing city, Huangqiao is lagging behind. With this initiative we hope to make more people to know Huangqiao and its immigrants' children primary school." It is obvious that the stark contrast between the lives of rural immigrants and that of urban middle class is the key stimulus.

Some of the artworks went beyond this preliminary goal of exposure and endeavored to criticize the developmentalist mode. The senses of bizarre, absurdity, insecurity, wound, etc. are explicit. The viaduct bridge under which the exhibition was displayed is officially owned by the municipal government, but in practice it is daily used by the local people for piling materials and keeping livestock's. Youngsters play billiard there too. For the purpose of the exhibition, it was wrapped around with hard plastic boards to form a make-shift "gallery". At the scene, it was dubbed as 'Lower Stratum Gallery' (Pinyin: *xiaceng jianzhu yishuguan*), a witty pun reflecting both its physical setting (under the viaduct) and its actual *chengzhongcun* resident users (since *xiaceng* also means lower class in Chinese).

Engaging a Chengzhongcun

In the section of installation at the Huangqiao exhibition, '*Death of a bicycle*' is a folding bike "accidentally" laid down inside white dashes mimicking traffic accident control lines. In recent years China has become a key market for automobiles, and the stereotype of China as a country on (two) wheels are getting obsolete. It was supposed to be an amazing experience to watch it under the viaduct bridge which is busy of traffic both day and night. Another installation is an intact chicken coop on the ground. The artist had gained consent from the owner to let it into the exhibition and most importantly left it as it was. Any audience with the knowledge of village evictions and displacement of villagers in urban regeneration, sometimes in a violent way, would have noticed the chicken and their coop (Fig. 5.2).

At a short distance, the wall in the school is covered by canvas printed with photos of deceased students in the 2008 Sichuan earthquake, names of social activists, and catch phrases from online forums such as on milk contamination scandal, etc. This "*Forgetting*" resonates to the other "*Finding Someone*", which is a series of photographs of children in poor rural areas. The photos are basically in black and white tones that blend

Fig. 5.2 Scenes at the Huangqiao exhibition (*Source* photographs by Mr. Wen Tong, May 8, 2010, Hefei, China. Reproduced with permission)

seamlessly with poverty-stricken image of rural China, while the visually disturbing distortion of facial parts of the rural children hints the bleak fate they are condemned to.

As Sullivan has pointed out, the exposure of "the sickness of modern Chinese urban society" and "the corrupting influence of burgeoning consumerism" is an important part of modern art in China (Sullivan, 1999). One of the performance arts is the "*Nightmare*". It was performed by a female volunteer naked and covered with decorative golden foil. She was escorted through the crowd holding a sizable "golden ore" while inviting the audience to touch or taste the "gold". But eventually the "gold" was dumped into an open sewage because it was merely a piece of well-wrapped stone. In the narrow lane that connects the "Lower Stratum Gallery" and the school a few auto showgirls were washing a BMW and would provide this service in exchange for "happiness". The blatant zero-sum trade between happiness and luxury reveals the dilemma inherent to the burgeoning fetishism of the Chinese *nouve-riches*.

In a more nuanced manner, earlier in the Huaihe Rd. shopping area a few hundred of itch-scratchers were distributed to passing-bys to "Let a few scratch itches first". It is doubtful that whether a parody to the famous motto "Let a few get rich first" from Deng Xiaoping in the early years of the reform was intended. Anyhow, participants were encouraged to pick the handy tool and use it as they wish: break it, sell it, throw it, dump it, share it with others, and above all when "Feeling unhappy? Scratch it!".

Likewise, the empowering trick was also adopted in the Huangqiao exhibition whereby small patches of cloths were freely distributed. Interesting enough, the design of this cloth features blossoming peonies and flying phoenixes on a red background. While that image used to be a genre motif of duvet cover that is popular in rural Hefei, it seems incompatible with the new urban lifestyle and is fading out quickly. The carnivalsque free sharing of cloth that embodies vernacular cultural tells as much about the nature of Chinese urbanism as its modern layouts. It testifies to the observation that "in post-Mao China, practices of nostalgia, revitalization, and reenchantment have taken up folk cultures from the countryside and worked them as malleable substances that can lend vitality and continuity in a swiftly changing, often disorienting, reform process" (Schein, 2003).

DELIBERATIVE DEMOCRACY: THE "EFFECT OF EFFECTS"

An Ephemeral Event?

When I visited Huangqiao *chengzhongcun* in July 2010, there were very few visible evidences that an art exhibition had taken place in the village. Apart from the graffiti on the bridge piers, there were not too many remnants of the "gallery", the performances, and the installations that had been set up for the "Huangqiao Happiness Project". Local residents said that they had been aware of the event, but that it had only left a small imprint on their minds. Naturally, it has to be questioned whether this event has generated any positive effects for the residents of Huangqiao and other *chengzhongcuns*. Did their situation improve because of the exposure caused by the exhibition? What can we learn from the process that involves the participation of the organizers, residents and audiences?

Actually, on the very same day of my visit, a group of students from Anhui University of Science and Technology visited Huangqiao as a part of their "Summer Social Practices" (Pinyin: *shuqi shehui shijian*) and donated three secondhand computers to the school (Fig. 5.3).

As a matter of fact, the curators had always downplayed the social and the political role of their exhibition. In-stead, they stressed the experimental character, the "playfulness" (Pinyin: *haowan*) and the artistic merit of the works on display. This stance and tone comes a long way toward the blurring of the actual motif of this event. But a closer read into the initiative stage reveals the aim. The choice to organize part of the exhibition in a *chengzhongcun* was not accidental. In an interview with the journalist of a local newspaper, one of the curators explained that the stark contrast between the life of the urban middle class and that of the rural immigrants had encouraged him to bring the exhibition to Huangqiao. "During our visit to the primary school," he said, "we saw the clash between the city and the countryside that came with the dramatic transformation of the Chinese economy and we came up with the concept of 'Huangqiao Happiness' project" (Feng et al., 2010). The other curator added that "Huangqiao is lagging behind the rest of the fast growing city" and that he hoped to "make more people know about Huangqiao and its immigrants' children primary school with his initiative" (ibid.). It is obvious that the social polarization that comes with fast urbanisation is the primary incentive.

The discourse on this event is packed into very ambiguous languages. Considering the social context where this event took place, it is a rather

Fig. 5.3 University students visiting the Huangqiao school (*Source* Photographs by the author, July 14, 2010, Hefei, China)

tactical manner of getting message through. Most of the mass media in China have a policy of self-censorship such that they could "bypass political 'minefields', and at the same time increase the possibility of the publication of reports on highly politically sensitive topics" (Tong, 2009, p. 594). There is a subtle balance to be kept between news reporting and political criticism of social consequences. It is equally true for other public events that have potential political implications such as this one. Its political criticism is kept underdeveloped, and whenever it comes to the motivation, the curators choose to be rather vague. For Zhang, the exhibition in Huangqiao was meant to be "a multi-dimensional and non-traditional exposure of both psychological and physical spaces" (Feng et al., 2010). Rather than a direct result, he hoped that the art on display would transmit an "effect of effects" in the psychology of the audiences. Even though he acknowledged that the precise shape of this effect was out of the control of the artists and the curators, he hoped that it would be related to democracy, social justice, and eventually happiness (Zhang, 2010b).

Virtual Space of Deliberations

Nonetheless, this "effect of effects" reminds us of deliberative democracy. The concept of deliberative democracy "refers to a specific form of participation: informed discussion between individuals about issues which concern them, leading to some form of consensus and collective decision" (Wright & Street, 2007, p. 850). Whatever the motivations of the audiences to participate, the exhibition managed to attract the attention from thousands of people visit Huangqiao or take part in the online discussions. More than 3,000 people visited Huangqiao on the first day alone. A few dozen of national and local media also covered the exhibition. One of the local news groups even made a short documentary for this event.

It is important to know how the participants saw this event. To this end, we apply Content Analysis to the discussion in online forums. As noted above, internet forums played an important role in the organization of this exhibition. Online forums are not only the meeting place for organizers and artists, but also a public tribune for those participated as audiences or commenter. As Li puts it, the internet in China has become the "social venues for the lower middle class and students" (Li, 2010, p. 64). On the other hand, considering its size, diversity, dynamic and ephemeral quality, and the textuality, interactivity and multimodality (Mautner, 2005, pp. 814–20), internet could be both an opportunity and a challenge for analysts. It is believed that internet could facilitate the deliberative democracy because of its accessibility, anonymity and asynchronous nature. In the case of the Hefei Biennale, we have selected Hefei Online (bbs.hefei,cc), one of the most popular local online forum in Hefei, for the case study. Since its founding in 2004, it has become one of the leading local gateway website of the city with more than 1.5 million registered users. Most of the discussions on the Hefei Biennale were found on this forum.

Figure 5.4 shows that these discussions continued after the event. The graph illustrates that Huangqiao received a lot of exposure on online forums. While the name of the village had only appeared in four threads of between 2006 and 2010, it was discussed rather extensively throughout 2010 and well into 2011. The amount of threats opened before the exhibition can be partly explained by the fact that online forums played an

'Huangqiao' in online forum bbs.hefei.cc

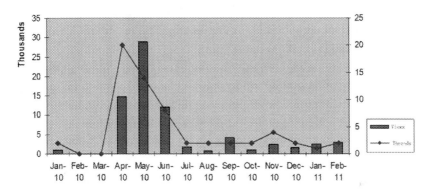

Fig. 5.4   Discussions on Huangqiao in a local online forum, 2010–2011 (*Source* Search engine used: www.google.com)

important role in the whole organization process of the biennale. Many participants also used online forums to publicise the event and to disseminate practical information. The rise after the exhibition has to do with debates after the event, however. In the weeks after the controversial exhibition, the art project, the village and the school received a lot of attention. In absolute numbers, threads which mentioned Huangqiao received more than 50,000 views.

Obviously, it has to be questioned what all this exposure eventually brought about. We would like to stress here that a closer look at the comments in online forums could tell some more insights of the nature of online discussions. First of all, the nature of the comments are rather complex. Most of them were written with plain language, although online slang or abbreviation is common place. Pun with homophonies is another linguistic feature. Sometimes it is believed as a tactic to bypass censorship, but the abuse of this trick is in fact in many cases a joyful game in itself. The style of online languages also includes the use of icons or figures in the place of characters. All of these characteristics have lead to some difficulties in reading the comments.

Secondly, the role of the organizers in the forums is not significant. One of the reasons is that the curators and artists were active in some other forums other than this local one. At least one of the organizers was active in the Hefei online forum as well to publicise this event. Posts that read like from the organizers are not received with special attention in terms of clicks or replies. Instead, individual netizens are more interested in third party reports. However, due to the anonymity of this forum, it can only be a conjecture that those posts are really from independent third party reporters rather than some of the organizers.

Moreover, most of the comments take a cynical/critical view of art and artists. Many of the audiences report that they are confused by the performance art, "couldn't comprehend" (Pinyin: *kan budong*) is a typical comment that reappear from time to time. Equally prominent is the criticism raised on the artistic achievement as many contend the whether the performance should be deemed as a kind of art. For instance, Tiandiyihao contends that "(the nudist performance is) really disgusting. (It) tarnishes the word of art" (posted by Tiandiyihao on 2010-6-9). The artists were in general badly mocked. Commenting on the nudist artist of the "Nightmare" performance, one claims that "simply by looking at her figure could I lose weight (because of vomiting)" (posted by Hongmingu on 2010-6-9).

Lastly, the attitude of the netizens toward the event skews to the negative side. In general the comments fail to reflect on either the artistic merits or the social political motives. An embarrassing fact is, however, most of them focus on the trivial and superficial facts such as free gifts or the physical figure of the artists. Some netizens suspect that it was merely "hype" for fame. There were a few posts that reflected on the motifs of the artworks, such as the satirical stance against social injustice and fetishism, but they were either dismissed or discarded. That being said, however, quite some of the commenter did express their interests in learning this event in their city.

Should the effect be seen from the interaction between artists and the audiences including the online commenter, this event has failed to reach out in the level of public art, let alone its political message. The tactical, and hence ambiguous, stance in the discourses used by the organizers, as well as the immense cultural gap between performance art and the folk culture of Chinese urban–rural interface areas, have to be blamed. The cynicism towards the artworks and the artists is not a real surprise. The single post that has attracted the highest attention is not on the artwork, but rather on the bleak conditions of the poor illegal school that was about to host the exhibition (posted by bwltw on 2010-4-29). The exposure certainly shocked many of the netizens: there were four inquiries (out of the 145 comments) on the exact location of the school in the following days. Many of the comments are mixed with grievance, surprise and compassion. Some commentators recalled their childhood schools and asked why such misery still exists nowadays. It even managed to attract some people who seem to be living around the village, as ErA wrote:

> It is all grievances in my heart whenever I pass by under the bridge in the evening. On the garbage-stricken path leading to Huangqiao, the smell is irritating. Thanks to the artists for the concern on Huangqiao. (You may) take bus No. 117, 4, 232, 46 or 7 and get off at Tankaungchang, and then walk northward for 30 meters under the bridge, then you will see the misery. How sad! Thanks again to all artists. (posted by ErA on 2010-5-2)

It is worth noting that most of the comments show clear support of the initiative with words or icons. One of the commenters openly called for "equality for education", while others suggest forwarding this thread to officials of the municipal government.

Indeed, although this event was far from seamless within cultural life of the city, it nevertheless goes beyond merely cultural influence. It allows the wide participation from art goers to village residents to internet users. Rather than transmitting a ready made message, it was organized for open debate. It provides a chance, a podium and a background for independent, and somehow contradictory, views. Public art is here both a subject and an object, and it the medium through which the aim of public attention is achieved. It is important because "participation as a right can be seen as a positive freedom which enables them to realize their social rights" (Gaventa, 2004, p. 30). In China where it is rather difficult to organize political campaigns even for basic social rights, the event is a genius initiative in combining public art with citizenship struggles.

It is by no means to say that events like this have the potential to solve the problem of citizenship in general. On the one hand, it has to be mentioned that Huangqiao *chengzhongcun* was demolished to make room for a real-estate development project. On the other hand, it also has to be noticed, however, that the problem of the illegal school has been addressed somehow. After the exhibition, education officials of the city of Hefei visited the school on a number of occasions. In a dialogue with the users of an online forum, they even promised to address its vulnerable situation. When Huangqiao *chengzhongcun* was demolished, all 123 students were transferred to public schools in nearby communities without extra charges. Recently, Hefei was even nominated to be one of the trial cities for the National Educational System Comprehensive Reforms. While former amendments still discriminated against children of immigrants, this reform aimed to define equal rights to education regardless of geographical background or *hukou*. For the first time in their lives, immigrant children shared the right to public education in the cities with their urban neighbors.

CONCLUSION

The Chinese citizenship deviates from the classical citizenship in the Western welfare states. While citizenship, embodied in the *hukou* system, has been institutionalized at a national level, however, a common nationality does not guarantee the Chinese nationals the same citizenship rights. Localized functions of the *hukou* system determine the social rights of citizens such as housing and education. The rural immigrants in the city, and especially the residents of *chengzhongcun*, are excluded from enjoying these rights. They are also more often than not in lack of enough social capital to organized effective resistance. Consequently, their struggle for citizenship rights calls for new strategies.

In this chapter I have examined a successful case using public arts in the struggle for education rights. The "Happiness Hefei" project raised the question of happiness at a time when Chinese cities are enjoying unprecedented prosperity. Against the predominate positivism, the other side of the development, i.e. the deprivation of rural immigrants and the future of their children, is at odds with the mainstream. To address this problem, a provocative strategy of bringing art into an impoverished community was adopted. Even if the curators had avoided of being straightforward in criticism, the exhibition had succeeded in creating an interruption to the lives and notions of ordinary urban middle class. As the thousands of audiences and even more online participants got involved in the action, they were at the same time the agent and object of a public pedagogy of citizenship rights.

Notwithstanding the "risks of simplistic celebration of romanicization" (Pinder, 2008, p. 733), public art has proved itself the potential in social intervention. By no means should one conclude that public art is capable to solve the citizenship problem alone. The parents of the children, for instance, would still find another *chengzhongcun* to stay if they can not afford an urban house on the market. Nonetheless, with the help of public arts, the underprivileged members of the society respond to social foes with satire, mocking, and most of all exposure. Public art appeals not to the authority to which citizenship is an instrument, but to the conscience and morality of the public such that a sense of solidarity, or in Biesta's word, "togetherness", could be forged.

Writing on civil society of China, Brook and Frolic note that "it is a process ... of citizenship within the context of public actions, including the obligation to voice dissent against unjust actions of the state" (Brook & Frolic, 1997). In transitional China, the interplay between governance, urban development, citizenship struggle, etc. are deeply intertwined. In the case of Huangqiao *chengzhongcun*, it is clear that the final solution to the education of immigrant children is a combination of public and private intervention. As the new reform of national education system proceeds, hopefully the future children of China would have the same right of education as bestowed by their citizenship. In this sense, this case is as much reflective to the past pitfalls as inspirational towards future citizenship struggles.

REFERENCES

Anonymous. (2010). The Hefei contemporary art biennale has made several "world records". Available at: http://news.sina.com.cn/c/2010-05-10/155 917488812s.shtml. Accessed June 5, 2011.
Berghuis, T. J. (2006). *Performance art in China*. Timezone8.
Biesta, G. (2006). What's the point of lifelong learning if lifelong learning has no point? On the democratic deficit of policies for lifelong learning. *European Educational Research Journal, 5*(3), 169–180. https://doi.org/10. 2304/eerj.2006.5.3.169
Biesta, G. (2012). Becoming public: Public pedagogy, citizenship and the public sphere. *Social & Cultural Geography, 13*(7), 683–697. https://doi.org/ 10.1080/14649365.2012.723736
Brook, T., & Frolic, B. M. (Eds.). (1997). *Civil society in China*. M.E. Sharpe.
Chen, Y. F. (Ed.). (2009). *Urban grand development: Political sociology of space production*. Shanghai Ancient Publishing Housing. [in Chinese].
Cheng, T., & Selden, M. (1994). The origin and social consequences of China's Hukou system. *The China Quarterly, 139*, 644–668. https://doi.org/10. 1017/S0305741000043083
Feng, J., Zhang, Y. P., Zhu, F., Liu, R., Xie, Z., Xu, F., Cao, H., & Bu, L. (2010). A 'happiness project' unfolded in Huangqiao. In Y. P. Zhang (Ed.),

Huangqiao happiness project 2010' Hefei contemporary art biennial: Art and literature. Yunhua Media, page numbers missing [in Chinese].

Froissart, C. (2009). The rise of migrant workers' collective actions: Toward a new social contract in China. In K. E. Kuah-Pearce & G. Guiheux (Eds.), *Social Movements in China and Hong Kong: The expansion of protest space* (pp. 155-178). Amsterdam University Press.

Gaventa, J. (2004). Towards participatory governance: Assessing the transformative possibilities. In S. Hickey & G. Mohan (Eds.), *Towards participation as transformation: Critical themes and challenges for a post-tyranny agenda* (pp. 25–41). Zed Books.

Grundy, J., & Boudreau, J. (2008). "Living with culture": Creative citizenship practices in Toronto. *Citizenship Studies, 12*(4), 347–363. https://doi.org/10.1080/13621020802184226

Gui, Y., Ma, W., & Muhlhahn, K. (2009). Grassroot transformation in contemporary China. *Journal of Contemporary Asia, 39*(3), 400–423. https://doi.org/10.1080/00472330902944487

Heisler, B. S. (1991). A comparative perspective on the underclass: Questions of urban poverty, race, and citizenship. *Theory and Society, 20*(4), 455–483. https://doi.org/10.1007/BF00157322

Holton, R. J. (2000). Multi-cultural citizenship. In E. F. Isin (Ed.), *Democracy* (pp. 189–202). Routledge.

Isin, E. F. (2009). Citizenship in flux: The figure of the activist citizen. *Subjectivity, 29*, 367–388. https://doi.org/10.1057/sub.2009.25

Isin, E. F., & Turner, B. S. (2007). Investing Citizenship: An agenda for citizenship studies. *Citizenship Studies, 11*(1), 5–17. https://doi.org/10.1080/13621020601099773

Kuah-Pearce, K. E., & Guiheux, G. (2009). Framing social movements in contemporary China and Hong Kong. In K. E. Kuah-Pearce & G. Guiheux (Eds.), *Social movements in China and Hong Kong: The expansion of protest space*. Amsterdam University Press.

Lawy, R., & Biesta, G. (2006). Citizenship-as-practice: The educational implications of an inclusive and relational understanding of citizenship. *British Journal of Educational Studies, 54*(1), 34–50. https://doi.org/10.1111/j.1467-8527.2006.00335.x

Lawy, R., Biesta, G., McDonnell, J., Lawy, H., & Reeves, H. (2010). "The art of democracy": Young people's democratic learning in gallery contexts. *British Educational Research Journal, 36*(3), 351–365. https://doi.org/10.1080/01411920902935808

Li, L., Li, S., & Chen, Y. (2010). Better city, better life, but for whom? The *hukou* and resident card system and the consequential citizenship stratification in Shanghai. *City, Culture and Society, 1*(1), 145–154. https://doi.org/10.1016/j.ccs.2010.09.003

RESISTANCE, PUBLIC ART AND CITIZENSHIP   117

Li, S. (2010). The online public space and popular ethos in China. *Media, Culture & Society, 32*(1), 63–83. https://doi.org/10.1177/016344370 9350098

Li, X. (2008). Analysis on the redevelopment of villages in the city. *Legality Tribune, 12*, 40–48. [in Chinese].

Liang, W., Hou, L., & Chen, W. (2008). Left-Behind children in rural primary schools: The case of Sichuan province. *Chinese Education and Society, 41*(5), 84–99. https://doi.org/10.2753/CED1061-1932410506

Lin, G. C. S. (2009). *Developing China: Land, politics and social conditions.* Routledge.

Liu, Z. (2009). Liushou children in a Chinese village: Childhood apart from parents. *Chinese Sociology and Anthropology, 41*(3), 71–89. https://doi.org/10.2753/CSA0009-4625410306

Marshall, T. H. (1950). *Citizenship and social class and other essays.* Cambridge University Press.

Mautner, G. (2005). Time to get wired: Using web-based corpora in critical discourse analysis. *Discourse & Society, 16*(6), 809–828. https://doi.org/10.1177/0957926505056661

Minty, Z. (2006). Post-apartheid public art in Cape Town: Symbolic reparations and public space. *Urban Studies, 43*(2), 421–440. https://doi.org/10.1080/00420980500406728

Morris, L. (1994). *Dangerous classes: The underclass and social citizenship.* Routledge.

Pinder, D. (2008). Urban interventions: Art, politics and pedagogy. *International Journal of Urban and Regional Research, 32*(3), 730–736. https://doi.org/10.1111/j.1468-2427.2008.00810.x

Reiter, B. (2009). Fighting exclusion with culture and art: Examples from Brazil. *International Social Work, 52*(2), 155–166. https://doi.org/10.1177/0020872808099727

Schein, L. (2003). Urbanity, Cosmopolitanism, Consumption. In N. N. Chen, C. D. Clark, S. Z. Gottschang, & L. Jeffery (Eds.), *China urban: Ethnographies of contemporary culture* (pp. 225–241). Duke University Press.

Sharp, J., Pollock, V., & Paddison, R. (2005). Just art for a just city: Public art and social inclusion in urban regeneration. *Urban Studies, 42*(5–6), 1001–1023. https://doi.org/10.1080/00420980500106963

Solinger, D. J. (1995). China's Urban transients in the transition from socialism and the collapse of the communist "urban public goods regime." *Comparative Politics, 27*(2), 127–146. https://doi.org/10.2307/422161

Solinger, D. J. (1999). *Contesting citizenship in urban China: Peasant migrants, the state and the logic of the market.* University of California Press.

Sullivan, M. (1999). Art in China since 1949. *The China Quarterly, 159*, 712–722. https://doi.org/10.1017/S0305741000003453

Tong, J. (2009). Press self-censorship in China: A case study in the transformation of discourse. *Discourse & Society, 20*(5), 593–612. https://doi.org/10.1177/0957926509106412

White, M. (2008). Can an act of citizenship be creative? In Engin. F. Isin & Greg M. Nielson (Eds.), *Acts of citizenship* (pp. 44–56). Zed Books.

Wiseman, M. B. (2007). Subversive strategies in Chinese avant-garde art. *The Journal of Aesthetics and Art Criticism, 65*(1), 109–119. https://doi.org/10.1111/j.1540-594X.2007.00242.x

Wright, S., & Street, J. (2007). Democracy, deliberation and design: The case of online discussion forums. *New Media & Society, 9*(5), 849–869. https://doi.org/10.1177/1461444807081230

Ye, P., & Xu, X. (2008). Measures for harmonious remodeling of the "village-in-city" in Hefei. *Journal of Hefei University of Technology, 31*(11), 1867–1871. [in Chinese].

Zhang, L. (2010a). The right to the entrepreneurial city in reform-era China. *The China Review, 10*(1), 129–155.

Zhang, Y. (2010b). *On "Huangqiao happiness project": Curator's note of the second Hefei contemporary art biennale of 2010.* Available at: http://www.imedia.com.cn/?uid-20-action-viewspace-itemid-14799. Accessed June 29, 2011.

Zhang, L., Zhao, S. X. B., & Tian, J. P. (2003). Self-help in housing and chengzhongcun in China's urbanization. *International Journal of Urban and Regional Research, 27*(4), 912–937. https://doi.org/10.1111/j.0309-1317.2003.00491.x

CHAPTER 6

Slum Tourism: Towards Inclusive Urbanism?

Abstract This chapter takes slum tourism as niche tourism and relates it to two cases of art-led *chengzhongcun* tourism in Guangzhou and Shenzhen. Instead of retrieving moral critiques, it is argued that slum tourism is a niche tourism that actively engages the slum community. Slum tourism has the right to exploit this market niche as long as consent is gained from local communities. The Chinese case takes a trajectory that is different from some renowned cases in other countries. The situation and strategy could vary greatly and yet they share similar effects. In the search for able agencies in community development, the potentialities of slum tourists as the agents of inclusive development should not be overlooked. It offer a democratic approach complimentary to conventional power apparatuses. More comparative studies between China and other countries in the Global South are needed.

Keywords Slum tourism · Morality · Slumming · Guangzhou · Shenzhen

INTRODUCTION

The slum in the developing world is becoming a new field for international tourism. Statistics from top destinations report that slum tourism

Y. Ding, *Urban Informal Settlements*,
https://doi.org/10.1007/978-981-16-9202-4_6

has quite a note worthy fraction of tourists ranging from a few thousands to hundreds of thousands (Freire-Medeiros, 2009; Meschkank, 2011; Rolfes, 2010; Rolfes et al., 2009). This emerging "extraordinary form of tourism", as Rolfes (2010: 438) put it, has provoked a lot of scholarly interests in recent years. Special attention has been given to the production of touristic space (Allen & Brennan, 2004; Freire-Medeiros, 2009), the ethics debate (Briedenhaan & Ramchander, 2006; Butcher, 2003; Selinger & Outterson, 2009), and the tour experiences (Ma, 2010; Meschkank, 2011; Rolfes, 2010; Rolfes et al., 2009). Slum-Tourism remains "extraordinary" despite the efforts to explain it as slum are not places normally associated with the positive connotations of tourism.

The cities of the developing world have to accommodate more than 95% of the net increase of world population (Grimm et al., 2008), a pressure that results in the proliferation of slums. In the eyes of the UN-Habitat, the slum is the "result of a failure of housing policies, laws and delivery systems, as well as of national and urban policies" (UN-Habitat, 2003a: 5). Despite the variations in physical settings and social contexts, a slum means lack of urban formalities in terms of infrastructure, social services, governance, employment, etc. It embodies many of the deficits that come along with urbanization and development, or rather the lack of development. It is predicted that the number of slum dweller worldwide will reach two billion by 2030 (United Nations, 2007).

The attitude toward slum tourism is quite polarized. Its proponents uphold the poverty alleviation function (Freire-Medeiros, 2009; Rogerson, 2004), whereas critics point to the troublesome ethics of slum tourism (Marrison, 2005; Weiner, 2008; Williams 2009; Rofles, 2010). In this chapter I explore a perspective on slum tourism that tries to transcend the dichotomy in asking whether slum tourism can be an agent of development. Can slum tourism support the struggle against the conditions of segregation, exclusion that many slums suffer from? Arguably the slum is a stage of great potential for interaction between slum tourists and slum residents. Slum tourism might provide a new route into development, especially at a time when existing agencies, such as inter-governmental organizations, NGOs, etc. are having difficulties to deliver effective and sustainable solutions. This chapter also contributes to the literature on slum-tourism by highlighting the phenomenon in a Chinese context. Previous studies on slum tourism have focused mainly on Brazil, South Africa and India. Given China's stage of development and the recent history of urbanization, it seems logical to ask if there is slum tourism in China, and if so, what does it look like? To answer these questions, it is necessary to form a comparative framework upon which slums are generalized to some extent. In this I understand slums as a general condition of modern urbanity. In this paper I introduce two Chinese cases that are related to slum tourism in one way or another.

In this chapter, I first confront the ambivalences of slum tourism by relating it to the notion of niche tourism. The second section focuses on the Chinese *chengzhongcun*, and tourism marketing strategies and regulations in China. Thirdly, two cases of the use of art in *chengzhongcun* tourism and *chengzhongcun* development are showcased. The chapter finishes with some arguments on the potentials and pitfalls of slum tourism in the making of an inclusive city.

SLUM TOURISM AS NICHE TOURISM

Is Slum Tourism Losing the Ethics Ground?

The slum is closely associated with the British urban history (Gilbert, 2007; Koven, 2004; Steinbrink, 2012). The recent incarnation of "slum tourism" has started in cities in developing countries in the early 1990s. Unlike in journalism, "slum tourism" as a term is seldom used in the academic world. This may be attributed to the fact that the term "slum" is contested. Given the geographical and linguistic variances across the globe, it is indeed a question to which extent the term slum can be considered as a universally valid description of places of urban poverty. Also travel agents often stick to the more specific "*favela* tour" or "township tour" rather than "slum tour" to market their products (Fig. 6.1). There are numerous names for slum-like communities around the world, each embedded in its peculiar social-cultural background. Attempts have been made to document the variations (for a table of place names equivalent to the slum, see UN-Habitat, 2003a: 60–75). For the sake of cross-cultural comparative studies, it is necessary to excavate "slum" from its historical background. Defining the global slum however is not easy amides a myriad of lived experiences of what could be described as slums.

The ethics critique deserves a bit more clarification. The growing interest in slum in recent years has resuscitated all the "inglorious associations" between the slum and its negative connotations (Gilbert, 2007). However, the critique on the ethics of slum tourism is not new. Ever since the early nineteenth century when the word "slum" was coined, more

Fig. 6.1 View inside a *favela* in São Paulo (*Source* Photo taken by the author on Aug. 23 2009, São Paulo, Brazil)

social and cultural layers have been added onto it such that the slum becomes a pejorative term characterized with dirt, poverty, and crime, etc. There is a danger that the misuse by journalists or social scientists of related terms, such as the *underclass*, as Gans (2007) argues, would lead to the stigmatization of certain groups and their respective spaces. The evolution from physical space to social space demonstrates how the "slum" is produced along with negative connotations.

The ambivalent nature of slum might have led researchers to eschew from using the term "slum tourism". Instead "poverty tourism" is widely used, however, while this term is certainly relevant to slum tourism, the substitution is not without problem. For instance, numerous sources have confirmed that the slum is not only a place of poverty, but also of genuine creativity and entrepreneurship. Some researchers have also noted some similarities between slum tourism and dark tourism (Freire-Medeiros, 2009; Rolfes et al., 2009). While the slum, despite its bleak

conditions, hardly overlaps with dark tourism destination, the two categories do converge on their concern of "contemporary morality" (Stone,
2009).

Taking Up the Niche

To indulge in ethics critique may not only be unnecessary, but also
distractive to community development on the ground. It is unnecessary
because the pursuit for a moral way of doing tourism, or for an ultimate
"Good Tourist" as Allen and Brennan put it, should be conditioned upon
a world citizenship which is, however, a "utopian thinking" (Allen &
Brennan, 2004: 183). Only a good citizen whose interest transcend the
local level and reaches the global level could qualify for a good tourist,
whose act is for the general good. Beauregard and Bounds also reject
the idea of a cosmopolitan citizenship for its "idealism greatly exceeds its
substance" (Beauregard & Bounds, 2000: 246). It is distractive because
the moralized stance may underestimate "the potential [of tourism] to
address poverty and inequality" and "the transformative economic development that could make a substantial difference to Third World societies"
(Butcher, 2003: 3).

Given the widely acknowledged social polarization in the developing
world, Selinger and Outterson have contested that "if it is harmful for
Rocinha residents to be confronted with wealth and inequality, poverty
tours are not the primary cause" (Selinger & Outterson, 2009: 21). The
fact that poverty is observed during the slum tour does not make the
tourists more immoral than the social dynamics and the stakeholders that
have created the slum in the first place. The critique on the voyeurism of
slum tourists is misleading because it takes the symptom as the epidemic,
and condemns the witness as the perpetrator.

Compared to conventional modes of mass tourism, slum tourism is
still a minor phenomenon. Its participants are fewer, and the duration
shorter. Most slum tours cater to small groups of tourists who take a short
excursion into the slum. In this sense, it reflects a move, as observed by
Marson, "from the old-style standardized rigid motivations of tourists to
a more unique approach where wants and needs are focused upon (and
consumers are willing to pay for) experiences that may be more adven-
turous and meaningful" (Marson, 2011: 9). In other words it is a shift
from mass tourism to niche tourism, which is more specific and diverse.
The slum itself is also a kind of niche. From a geographical point of view,

the slum in China sometimes is located on the fringe of the city and is characterized with an intermingled landscape of the urban and the rural. Indeed, the slum belongs to and depends on the city, and yet it is not recognized as the city. The idea of the niche even goes beyond the spatial dimension. Given the close association with rural–urban migrants and the social and economic exclusion, the slum is a niche in not only spatially but also—and perhaps even more—in a socio-economic sense.

Contrary to the critique of voyeurism, tourism helps to rediscover these forgotten places of social exclusion and spatial segregation and to make them visible. Without the tourists, the slum would only be a marginalized place in the *established* spatial and social order. The presence of tourists is a disturbance of the normality. It is due to the special interests of some niche market tourists that this peculiar space of contemporary urbanity is known, seen and discussed. In this sense, I argue that slum tourism is niche tourism.

SLUM AND SLUM TOURISM IN CHINA: MEDIA, MARKETING AND MANAGEMENT

Whether "slums" exist in China is a delicate question. For instance, China is absent from a popular world slum distribution map (Ma, 2010). According to the official government line, slums were phased out from Chinese cities after the Socialist revolution. By securing urban employment and social housing, the eradication of the slum was hailed as a great achievement in the late 1950s. However, in reality housing shortage remained a constant phenomenon in Chinese cities. Especially since the reforms in the 1980s, hundreds of millions of rural migrants have poured into the city. According to the UN-Habitat, China has a slum population of 178 million, which accounts for 37.8% of the total urban population (UN-Habitat, 2003b: 38). On the other hand, the World Bank has found that "the slums and endemic poverty that have taken root in other countries are largely absent from Chinese cities thus far." (Yusuf & Nabeshima, 2008: 27).

The type of community in Chinese city that is most comparable with the idea of a slum is the *chengzhongcun*. Wu et al. confronts the *chengzhongcun* (in their lexicon: urbanized village) with the criteria of slum identification adopted by the UN-Habitat and other scholars, and accepts the technical use of "slum" but refrains from the general usage since there are significant differences, i.e. mode of housing construction and land ownership, between the "urbanized village" and the slum (Wu et al., 2011: 8–9). I agree with Wu et al. that the social context in which the terms are applied should always be noted. But for practical reasons, in the rest of this paper *chengzhongcun* is used interchangeably with "slum".

The concept of "slum tourism" was introduced to China by journalism in the beginning of 2007 when Lu, a journalist, wrote about favela tours in Rio (Lu, 2007). In general, Chinese reports take a neutral attitude since slum tourism is deemed as a foreign issue, and very few have attempted to explore the link between slum tourism and the Chinese context (Tan, 2009). Forms of slum tourism as they have developed in Brazil, South Africa and India (e.g. guided tours, B&B) do not exist in China. There are several reasons behind this.

First of all, it is very difficult for the *chengzhongcun* to get official sanction and endorsement. Tourism in China is overseen by the tourism office who determines whether a place can be a legal touristic destination or not. The *Management Regulations of Tourism Development and Planning*, issued by the National Tourism Agency of China, orders that "tourism development and planning should be in accordance with national land use planning, [local] comprehensive land use planning, urban master plan, etc." (National Tourism Agency of China, 2000: sec. 3, art. 12). Due to the fast urbanization in recent decades, the *chengzhongcun* is under constant threat of eviction and redevelopment which rules out the possibility of long term tourism planning. Chinese officials tend to take a developmentalist view on urban issues. Unlike the Brazilian president Lula who openly endorsed the *favela* tour (Hestbaek, 2010), there is no support for *chengzhongcun* tourism from higher level officials in China except for a few cases such as in the city of Shenzhen.

From the perspective of tourism marketing, the *chengzhongcun* does not have a strong relevance in Chinese tourism. For domestic tourists, a short excursion to the suburban countryside is widely known as 'nongjiale' [literally, farm joy] (He et al., 2004). But in practice it is a kind of rural retreat to the agricultural village and has nothing to do with the slum. To international tourists, poverty or slum has never been a main tourist attraction of China. Studies on the image and text in tourism promotion, i.e. travel brochures, reveal that the conventional attractions of China are "ruins", "religious sites", "palaces", "monuments" and "city gateways" etc. Accordingly, China is a destination to admire and meditate, rather than explore and discover (Echtner & Prasad, 2003). It is interesting to note that among the travel logs on four Chinese destinations, none of the tourists mention a word of slum or urban poverty (Hsu et al., 2009).

That being said, however, slum tourism is not irrelevant to China. As early as the beginning of twentieth century, Chinatowns in the US had been frequented as picturesque ethnical ghettos (Steinbrink, 2012; Williams, 2009). There was "ethnic slumming" in Chinatowns, but in Chinese towns there was no slumming. It's only recently that some of the Chinese urban policy makers are interested in taking the *chengzhongcun* into comprehensive tourism planning. For instance, in the city of Shenzhen, the redevelopment policy of *chengzhongcun* has set the goal of integration in four dimensions: spatial integration, management integration, economic integration and cultural integration (Urban Planning, Land and Resources Commission of Shenzhen Municipality, 2005). In terms of the cultural integration, it is emphasized that the "valuable cultural relics" and "good native cultural traditions" shall be protected. In 2009, the municipal government of Shenzhen city issued a set of guidelines to promote creative industry developments in which the *chengzhongcun* is given special supportive policy within the framework of urban regeneration. The *chengzhongcun* is encouraged to diversify its function so that it can catch up with urban development, and eventually attract investors and tourists from China and abroad.

Chinese researchers have attempted to examine the chance of promoting tourism in the *chengzhongcun*. Working on the touristic city of Kunming, Shi and Wen proposed a strategy to convert ethnic *chengzhongcuns* into scenic areas in accordance to local tourism planning (Shi & Wen, 2009). Urban experts and journalists have long been calling for new mentalities of incorporative development that aims not only to govern but also to serve the *chengzhongcun* (Liu, 2007). The interest in the *chengzhongcun* has increased in every level of the society. People from various backgrounds such as artists, architects, businessmen and scholars, etc. are attracted by the *chengzhongcun*. For instance, the pioneering Second Guangzhou Triennial of 2005, under the theme of "Alternative: Space of Special Modern Experiments", was the first art exhibition ever to dedicate a special session to the *chengzhongcun*.

ART-LEAD SLUM TOURISM AS AN ALTERNATIVE

A central question for slum tourism research is concerned with the reasons why tourists want to see the slum. During their fieldwork in Cape Town,

Rolfes, Steinbrink and Uhl found that "interest in local culture and people" was ranked the first in a group of six options (Rolfes, 2010; Rolfes et al., 2009). Similarly, Ma concludes from fieldwork in Dharavi, Mumbai that "cultural curiosity" is the primary cause to slum tourists (Ma, 2010). Arguably the slum might be seen as attractive because it appears to be the 'other' of modernity and globality (Steinbrink, 2012).

Chinese tourism is deeply embedded into its historical and cultural settings. The tourism sites in China are also made to accommodate this demand, for instance, new scenic projects would choose to promote Buddhist pilgrimages to attract tourists (Li, 2003). The *chengzhongcun* does not fit in with traditional cultural picture. Most of the *chengzhongcuns* were former agricultural villages, which were built with no anticipation of upcoming tourists in mind. The cultural capital of the *chengzhongcun* destination can either be found in the remnants of the rural past or in some new attractions resulting from its location in the city.

In the next section two intriguing cases of art-lead slum tour in China are introduced. Clearly they differ from the slum tourism model of some other countries. Even within China, these pioneering cases reveal how diverse the situations can be.

Times Museum: An Unusual Perspective

The Times Museum (Pinyin: *shidai meishuguan*) of Guangzhou is a private art museum. It is important not least for the fact that it is the second work of the Harvard-based architect Rem Koolhas in China (Zi & Xu, 2010). The museum is revolutionary in its hybrid space usage. There is no single building for this museum. Instead, it is embedded into an ordinary residential building. The museum consists of several floors in a high-rise apartment tower. The space on different floors is connected by independent elevators, thus it gives the whole museum a "T" structure (City Pictorial, 2011). It carves out certain floors to maximize the options of view points. For instance, seeing from the windows or the balcony or the two glasshouses in the exhibition hall, "visitors could have a bird's view of the city landscape of northern Guangzhou, which is a typical yet distinctive Chinese urban–rural coverage [sic] area" (Times Museum 2011). It is a rather euphemistic expression to call the neighboring *chengzhongcun* "urban–rural coverage area". Typically, residential projects like the one the museum belongs to are built on the outskirt of the city to meet the need of space and yet not to exceed the afford-ability of middle class customers. The compromise results in the intrusion of gated communities into the *chengzhongcun* area. To reach the Times Museum from the nearest metro station, for example, you need to cross the lanes of the neighboring *chengzhongcun* (City Pictorial, 2011).

Although the Times Museum is not built in the *chengzhongcun*, it provides an extraordinary way of engaging with the city. Unlike ordinary art museums, it is not just meant for urban cultural amenity. Rather, it stands as a unique "urban observatory" of the dynamism between the city and the "Other", i.e. the *chengzhongcun*. While the favela is probably the best place in Rio for beach views, in Guangzhou it is the *chengzhongcun* that constitutes a middle class gaze. As the city expands, the contrast and struggle between the two types of residence is jarring. Although the *chengzhongcun* may retreat in future, at the moment the museum offers a panoramic view of the evolution of the city without the stress of going into the *chengzhongcun*. Since the opening in 2010, the Times Museum has quickly become a popular cultural attraction of the city and artists like Ou Ning and his partners have chosen it for their exhibitions on reform and rebuilding of rural communities (Ou, 2011).

Dafen: Place Making via Art Business

If art was a catalyst in the Huangqiao case (see Chapter 5), then it should only be called a driving force in the case of Dafen. Art never stops in the Dafen Oil Painting Village. In a city of hundreds of *chengzhongcuns*, Dafen village is the gem of Shenzhen and a must-go for many visitors. A local urban legend says that a businessman from Hong Kong came to Dafen in 1989 in favor of its low rents. At that time Dafen was still a predominately agricultural village like many other *chengzhongcuns* in Shenzhen. The business started with the recruitment of a few painters to work in Dafen and the products were then exported via Hong Kong SAR. The painters were commissioned to make copies of well recognized Western oil painting masterpieces. It turned out to be a lucrative business such that many more businessmen and painters followed suit. At the turn of the century, original work also started to emerge in the market and nowadays it contributes a significant part in the turnovers. It was not easy to break the stereotype of copy making, but the shift toward original works has been proved to be a right direction (Tinari, 2007).

Over the last two decades, Dafen has become a nodal in the global oil painting market. It is said to be home to more than "800 galleries and over 5000 artists" (Dafen Village, 2008). The high demand from the oversea market of counterfeit "masterpieces" financially supported Dafen transformation. The local government has made great efforts to improve the working and living environment for art workers. Start-up artists, for instance, could manage to stay in the village thanks to the affordable housing project. In 2007, the one hundred million RMB (roughly equals ten million euro) project of Dafen Art Museum was completed. The scale of the museum (built-up area: 16,000 square meters) has made it probably the most sizable art museum ever built for a *chengzhongcun*. It is a public building at the extreme. "Anyone who comes to Dafen, businessmen, art collectors or other tourists, can drop in for a visit. "You can even contact the painter and settle a deal via the Museum if you are interested", said a painter in an interview (see: Huang, 2010). Every year tens of thousands of visitors frequent the lanes and the square of Dafen.

It would be difficult for visitors to associate Dafen with a slum. In terms of the ambiance, it resembles to the British planning concept of "urban village" to some extent. Interestingly it is promoted as a model of urban regeneration as well as "rural tourism". In accordance to the promotion campaign of "2006 Year of Rural Tourism", organized by the National Tourism Agency of China, Dafen was designated as one of the five pilot villages in the program "Shenzhen Rural Tour" (Wang, 2006). On the other hand in 2010, Dafen was invited to participate in the Best Urban Practices quarter of the 2010 Shanghai EXPO, representing the city of Shenzhen. Dafen Art Museum was the only participating site of its kind that is not located in the EXPO Park in Shanghai. Recent reports continually confirm that Dafen is one of the most popular tourism destinations in Shenzhen (Dafen Village, 2011).

TOWARDS THE INCLUSIVE CITY

The Millennium Development Goals (MDGs) of the United Nations, i.e. improving the living conditions of 100 million slum residents, has ended with limited success. Alan Gilbert (2007) was right to be skeptical on the legitimacy of inter-governmental initiatives. There is *no* one single strategy for all the slum problems of the world. The formidable challenge of the slum should be addressed in many ways, and tourism might be considered as one of them. Tourists are important representatives from the civil society and the act of tourism has the potential to work as dialogue between the visiting and the host societies. Moreover, tourism is a performative act that engages its environment in different stages, "the same tourist may act out a medley of roles during a single tour or holiday" (Edensor, 2000: 341). If we take the slum as one of the many stages for tourists, then they are able to bring something into the otherwise segregated and excluded slum community. Empirical studies have rejected the presumption that slum tourists are unwanted or not welcome. The "friendliness of residents" is the most important impression of the tourists (Rolfes, 2010; Rolfes et al., 2009). Ma also observed that "neutral" toward the tour is the typical attitude of slum residents. They didn't report resent to the tourist, quite on the contrary, the slum residents expect more interaction in the tour rather than simply "stop and look" (Ma, 2010). As long as the tour could obtain "community consent" on the basis of "democratic structures", there is no reason to object it (Selinger & Outterson, 2009).

Favela tourism proponents claimed that it helps the community "not only includes sanitation systems and other basic infrastructure, but emphasizes the importance of integrating the *favelas* both spatially and socially" (Freire-Medeiros, 2009: 581). Should we take comprehensive integration as the target of social development, communication and contact are vital to this process. Therefore, "being exposed", as proclaimed by the urbanist Peter Marcuse, is not a problem, but rather the first step to the "right to the city" (Peter Marcuse, in Horlitz & Vogelpohl, 2009). The criticism on tourists' voyeurism is not always a negative matter. Writing on the curious emotion, shame, Tucker argues that it "should be seen as positive in its reflexive and self-evaluative role" (Tucker, 2009: 455). In the context of international tourism, it helps the tourists "to engage ethically in 'doing tourism'" (ibid.). Due to this engaging power, slum tourism has the potential to act as the stimulating agency for a more inclusive urban policy.

DISCUSSION

In this paper I have taken a critical look at slum tourism in China. Instead of retrieving moral critiques, I argue for a new perspective to view slum tourism as niche tourism, a type of tourism that actively engages the slum community. The slum is the niche for the marginalized population, especially the immigrants, in the city. Slum tourism has a right to exploit this market niche as long as consent is gained from local communities. Thanks to the performative nature of tourism, the potentialities of slum tourists as the agents of inclusive development should never be overlooked. Tourism can offer a democratic approach complimentary to conventional power apparatuses such as governments, NGOs and international organizations.

To demonstrate the practicability of slum tourism, two cases from China were described here. They revealed that the situation and strategy could vary greatly and yet they share similar effects. In Dafen the tourists come only after an initial period of business development. They are not the decisive force in this process, but they could help to sustain the success of Dafen and perhaps even the transformation of it. Contrary to the rule of seeing slum tour as a kind of urban tourism, Dafen was intentionally promoted as a rural tourism destination. It reminds tourists of its rural origin, of course, but the current situation in Dafen also reveals the diversity and complexity of the *chengzhongcun* tourism, or even slum tourism in general (Frenzel & Koens, 2012). The case of Times Museum is rather ambiguous. Although from the outset it was expected to form a unique viewpoint of urban development, the very same process of development could undermine the view that is so vital to its uniqueness. If someday it is encircled by high-rise buildings, it will lose one of its most important treasures. Tourists to the Times Museum may not even be aware that they have been led into a designed spatial framework of social engagement, yet their very presence has made the *chengzhongcun* relevant to the city.

Research agenda on deprivation and poverty of the Global South has drifted from causal analysis of colonial and post-colonial power relationships to practical poverty alleviation strategies. In the search for able agencies in community development, slum tourism provides a valuable alternative. It's worthy noting that the contribution of slum tourism is far more profound than "creation of full-time or casual work opportunities" (Rogerson, 2004: 253). As far as China in concerned, slum tourism has been actively engaging with community developments. Besides, the Chinese case takes a trajectory that is different from some renowned cases in other countries. Nonetheless, they share some fundamental similarities. I end this chapter with a call for more comparative studies between China and other countries in the Global South.

REFERENCES

Allen, G., & Brennan, F. (2004). *Tourism in the New South Africa*. I.B. Tauris.

Anonymous. (2010). *The Hefei contemporary art biennale has made several "world records"*. http://news.sina.com.cn/c/2010-05-10/155917488812s. shtml. Accessed June 5, 2011.

Beauregard, R., & Bounds, A. (2000). Urban citizenship. In E. Islin (Ed.), *Democracy, citizenship, and the global city*. Routledge.

Briedenhaan, J., & Ramchander, P. (2006). Township tourism: Blessing or blight? The case of Soweto in South Africa. In M. K. Smith & M. Robinson (Eds.), *Cultural tourism in a changing world: Politics* (pp. 124–142). Channel View Publications.

Butcher, T. (2003). *The moralisation of tourism: Sun, sand…and saving the world?* Routledge.

City Pictorial. (2011). The times museum of Guangdong: Suspending on the air, hided in a residence. *City Pictorial*, No. 273/274, pp. 98–101 [in Chinese].

Dafen Village. (2008). Guanyu Dafen [about Dafen]. http://www.cndafen. com/about.asp?Title=关于大芬. Accessed June 8, 2011.

Dafen Village. (2011). *Dafen oil painting village nominated for the best cultural tourism route*. http://www.cndafen.com/shownews.asp?id=753. Accessed June 8, 2011.

Echtner, C. M., & Prasad, P. (2003). The context of third world tourism marketing. *Annals of Tourism Research, 30*(3), 660–682. https://doi.org/ 10.1016/S0160-7383(03)00045-8

Edensor, T. (2000). Staging tourism: Tourists as performers. *Annals of Tourism Research, 27*(2), 322–344. https://doi.org/10.1016/S0160-7383(99)000 82-1

Freire-Medeiros, B. (2009). The favela and its touristic transits. *Geoforum, 40*(4), 580–588. https://doi.org/10.1016/j.geoforum.2008.10.007

Frenzel, F., & Koens, K. (2012). Slum tourism: Developments in a young field of interdisciplinary tourism research. *Tourism Geographies, 14*(2), 195–212. https://doi.org/10.1080/14616688.2012.633222

Gans, H. J. (2007). Remembering the Urban villagers and its location in intellectual time: A response to Zukin. *City & Community, 6*(3), 231–236. https:// doi.org/10.1111/j.1540-6040.2007.00215_1.x

Gilbert, A. (2007). The return of the slum: Does language matter? *International Journal of Urban and Regional Research, 31*(4), 697–713. https://doi.org/ 10.1111/j.1468-2427.2007.00754.x

Grimm, N. B., Faeth, S. H., Golubiewski, N. E., Redman, C. L., Wu, J., Bai, X., & Briggs, J. M. (2008). Global change and the ecology of cities. *Science, 319*, 756–760. https://doi.org/10.1126/science.1150195

He, J., Li, H., & Wang, Q. (2004). Rural tourism in China: A case study of Nongjiale in the Chengdu metropolitan area. *Mountain Research and Development, 24*(3), 260–262. https://doi.org/10.1659/0276-4741(2004)024 [0260:RTIC]2.0.CO;2

Hestbaek, C. (2010, October 12). Rio top tour helping favela business. *The Rio Times.* http://riotimesonline.com/brazil-news/rio-business/poverty-safari-or-fabulous-favelas/. Accessed August 30, 2011.

Hsu, S., Dehuang, N., & Woodside, A. G. (2009). Storytelling research of consumers' self-reports of urban tourism experiences in China. *Journal of Business Research, 62*(2), 1223–1254. https://doi.org/10.1016/j.jbusres.2008.11.006

Horlitz, S., & Vogelpohl, A. (2009). Something can be done!—A report on the conference 'Right to the City, prospects for critical urban theory and practice', Berlin November 2008. *International Journal of Urban and Regional Studies, 33*(4), 1067–1072. https://doi.org/10.1111/j.1468-2427.2009.00931.x

Huang, J. (2010, November 11). The road toward art and internationalisation of a village in the city. *Chinese Cultural Daily* [in Chinese].

Koven, S. (2004). *Slumming: Sexual and social politics in Victorian London.* Princeton University Press.

Li, Y. (2003). Development of the Nanshan cultural tourism zone in Hainan, China: Achievements made and issues to be resolved. *Tourism Geographies, 5*(4), 436–445. https://doi.org/10.1080/1461668032000129155

Liu, Y. (2007, September 11). Focusing on slum from the perspective of culture services. *Shenzhen Business Daily* [in Chinese].

Lu, Y. (2007). Step into the favela of the second largest city in Brazil, Rio de Janeiro. *China Radio Internationa.* http://gb.cri.cn/14558/2007/01/31/1865@1430137.htm. Accessed June 12, 2011.

Ma, B. (2010). *A trip into the controversy: A study of slum tourism travel motivations.* 2009–2010 Penn Humanities Forum on Connections. http://repository.upenn.edu/uhf_2010/12. Accessed June 8, 2011.

Marrison, J. (2005). Wise to the streets. *The Guardian.* http://www.guardian.co.uk/travel/2005/dec/15/argentina.buenosaires.darktourism?INTCMP=SRCH. Accessed August 30, 2011.

Marson, D. (2011). From mass tourism to niche tourism. In P. Robinson, S. Heitmann, & P. Dieke (Eds.), *Research themes for tourism* (pp. 1–15). CAB International.

Meschkank, J. (2011). Investigations into slum tourism in Mumbai: Poverty tourism and the tensions between different constructions of reality. *GeoJournal, 76,* 47–62. https://doi.org/10.1007/s10708-010-9401-7

National Tourism Agency of China. (2000). *Management regulations of tourism development and planning.* http://www.gov.cn/gongbao/content/2001/content_61024.htm. Accessed August 30, 2011.

Ou, N. (2011). *Bishan project at Guangzhou times museum.* http://www.altern ativearchive.com/ouning/article.asp?id=834. Accessed June 22, 2011.

Rogerson, C. M. (2004). Urban tourism and small tourism enterprise development in Johannesburg: The case of township tourism. *GeoJournal, 60,* 249–257. https://doi.org/10.1023/B:GEJO.0000034732.58327.b6

Rolfes, M., Steinbrink, M., & Uhl, C. (2009). *Townships as attraction: A case study on township tourism in Cape Town.* http://www.geographie.uni-osnabr ueck.de/uploads/Steinbrink_Township.pdf. Accessed June 8, 2011.

Rolfes, M. (2010). Poverty tourism: Theoretical reflections and empirical findings regarding an extraordinary form of tourism. *GeoJournal, 75,* 421–442. https://doi.org/10.1007/s10708-009-9311-8

Selinger, E., & Outterson, K. (2009). *The ethics of poverty tourism.* Boston University School of Law Working Paper No. 09–29. http://www.bu.edu/law/faculty/scholarship/workingpapers/2009.htmal. Accessed May 22, 2011.

Shi, M., & Wen, Z. (2009). A tourism-lead urbanization approach to the chengzhongcun regeneration in Kunming. *Science & Techonology Information, 34,* 389–390 [in Chinese].

Steinbrink, M. (2012). 'We did the slum!' - Urban poverty tourism in historical perspective. *Tourism Geographies, 14*(2), 213–234. https://doi.org/10.1080/14616688.2012.633216

Stone, P. R. (2009). Dark tourism: Morality and new moral spaces. In R. Sharpley & P. R. Stone (Eds.), *The darker side of travel: The theory and practice of dark tourism* (pp. 56–72). Channel View Publications.

Tan, S. (2009). Show off happiness in the slum. *New Weekly,* No. 295, pp. 70–73 [in Chinese].

Times Museum. (2011). *About us.* http://www.timesmuseum.org/about/. Accessed June 12, 2011.

Tinari, P. (2007). Original copies: The Dafen oil painting village. *Art Forum International, 46*(2), 344–351. https://www.artforum.com/print/200708/original-copies-the-dafen-oil-painting-village-15882. Accessed June 12, 2011.

Tucker, H. (2009). Recognizing emotion and its postcolonial potentialities: Discomfort and shame in a tourism encounter in Turkey. *Tourism Geographies, 11*(4), 444–461. https://doi.org/10.1080/14616680903262612

UN-Habitat. (2003a). *Developing a set of indicators to monitor the full and progressive realisation of the human right to adequate housing.* https://www.un.org/ruleoflaw/blog/document/monitoring-housing-rights-develo ping-a-set-of-indicators-to-monitor-the-full-and-progressive-realisation-of-the-human-right-to-adequate-housing/. Accessed September 9, 2011.

UN-Habitat. (2003b). *The challenge of slums: Global report on human settlement 2003.* https://unhabitat.org/the-challenge-of-slums-global-report-on-human-settlements-2003. Accessed September 9, 2011.

United Nations. (2007). *Slum dwellers to double by 2030: Millennium development goal could fall short.* https://news.un.org/en/story/2003/10/81152-urban-slum-dwellers-could-double-2-billion-2030-un-agency-says.   Accessed September 9, 2011.

Urban Planning, Land and Resource Commission of Shenzhen Municipality. (2005). *Comprehensive plan for chengzhongcun regeneration of Shenzhen municipality: 2005–2010* [in Chinese].

Wang, Y. (2006, March 9). Chengzhongcun joins special tourism routes. *Southern Metropolis Daily* [in Chinese].

Weiner, E. (2008, March 9). Slum visits: Tourism or voyeurism? *The New York Times.* https://www.nytimes.com/2008/03/09/travel/09heads.html. Accessed August 30, 2011.

Williams, S. (2009). *Tourism geography: A new synthesis.* Routledge.

Wu, F., Zhang, F., & Webster, C. (2011). *Informality and 'slum clearance': The development and demolition of urbanized villages in the Chinese Peri-urban area.* Draft conference paper. http://www.rc21.org/conferences/amsterdam 2011/edocs2/Session%2029/29-1-Wu.pdf. Accessed September 2, 2021.

Yusuf, S., & Nabeshima, K. (2008). Optimizing urban development. In S. Yusuf & T. Saich (Eds.), *China urbanizes: Consequences, strategies, and policies* (pp. 1–40). The World Bank.

Zi, L., & Xu, L. (2010, December 16). Times Museum was actually a work of Rem Koohas. *Southern Metropolis Daily* [in Chinese].

CHAPTER 7

Conclusion

Abstract This concluding chapter challenges the idea that the Chinese case alone constitutes an independent entity from which urban theory could be derived. The *chengzhongcun*, for example, could only be comprehended in relation to similar or not-so-similar communities that may be located in far-flung places across the globe. Similarly, David Faure's scepticism on urbanism is rejected. *Chengzhongcun* is a transitory phenomenon in China's urbanisation process. It is emphasized that rather than being ambivalent or even denial towards urbanism, China should focus on embracing urbanism and eventually building an immunity of it.

Keywords Indigenization · Soviet urbanism · Hong Kong · Ding Right · Immunity

> *It [the rural component of Chinese civilization], and not the cities, defined the Chinese way of life.* (Mote, 1977: 105)

URBAN CHINA IN A NUTSHELL

"American Dream is dominated by low-density living", so writes Herbert J. Gans in his study on the post-war Levittowners (Gans, 1982: vii). But who doesn't, conditions permit, like low-density and yet reasonably convenient suburban communities? Does it really matter how it is called, urban village or Levittown? This preference, I believe, been engineered into human mind. After all, human body still bears the imprints of the hunt-gathering (including fishing) and sedentary agricultural civilisations. The simple fact is that, in modern market economies, people live in high density buildings or dilapidated areas not because they prefer it that way but because they have little alternatives.

While I concur with Tang's critique on the random indigenization and appropriation of Western concepts and theories, and uncritically apply them in urban China studies, I don't share his optimism in a "full-fledged Chinese theory" (Tang, 2019b: 482). And I doubt if that will ever make any sense. Throughout this study, I have had in mind the uncanny associations between the cases that are located in far-flung places across the globe, and relate the *chengzhongcun* to similar or not-so-similar communities. Core to this study is how to posit the *chengzhongcun* into a mosaic of global urbanism. It has to be reiterated that the aim of this effort is not to promote the cross-cultural transfer and transplantation of concepts or theories, important as it is, but rather to facilitate the "navigation" in a sea of variegated urbanism. But even with a good map or chart, precaution is needed in path finding.

During the years when this doctoral study was being made, the world reached the symbolic threshold of 50% urbanisation. However, there was no celebration about it. The world has been busily occupied with other matters. But there is probably also another reason to explain the indifference, namely there is not much novelty in the fact of urbanisation. Since most of the human beings are nowadays urban creatures, it is assumed that people know about the city, hence there is no special need to reexamine the way that city living is made possible. For instance, the great shift in human habitation has hardly resulted in any tangible change in terms of daily life. The institutions that guided the urban development before are still in effect today and are very likely to be also effective tomorrow.

That being said, the transition from rural to urban habitation is a daily fact to hundreds of millions of people, mostly in developing countries. It also explains why the *chengzhongcun* is special: because *chengzhongcun* is the place where the rural to urban transition is happening on a daily basis and at a scale probably unparalleled in human history. Compared to the disciplined city, the rural remnants of the *chengzhongcun* are not only reflected in poverty or physical degradation, but also in its social openness to low-income rural migrants.

It sounds ironic that it was not the city that opened its gates to its rural compatriots, but the village. On the other hand, it was not always an intentional choice of the *chengzhongcun* to become a migrant village. It has to do so in order to sustain its livelihood in an urbanising society. The role of the suburban village changed from providing food, in grain or in other forms, to providing space to the city. Once the condition is ripe, the *chengzhongcun* will be completely assimilated into the city in a way that it cancels itself: the village is dismantled and the inhabitants are relocated. To the migrants, however, the *chengzhongcun* acts as the entry point to the city thanks to the "in and yet out" character. The fact of living inside the *chengzhongcun* is an outcome and indicator of their marginal position in the urban society. What the immigrants are in lack of is not only financial means, notwithstanding being the most likely target for them, but also equal citizenship rights in order to enter the city.

Borrowing from Doreen Massey's analysis of regional development, later labeled as "geological metaphor", Kesteloot proposed to analyse the Chinese city as a geological metaphor, whereby the evolution in modes of production and their constitutive social groups produces different spatial configurations in the city. Just like geological layers, these configurations are resilient because of the life-time of the built environment (Kesteloot, 2004). This theory gives a historical dimension to urban development, which is often invisible or hard to discern, without knowledge of the history of urban development. From this point of view, the *chengzhongcun* might be taken as a cross-section sample of the whole urbanization process in China.

That has perhaps summarized the dynamics that have been driving the urbanisation process in China since the reform. No doubt this one is a scaled-down thematic study, but the time span of this study is not limited to very recent history, nor is the geographical location fixed to China. Unlike the British urban village movement, the *chengzhongcun* of China share more common ground with the Gansian urban village. Interesting enough, Gans did not stop at the West End type of "Urban Village" studies. His further research extended to include suburban New Towns such as the Levittown. His later works continued to shed light on the new forms of social marginalization of certain groups discriminated on the basis of income, race, or culture (Gans, 1990, 2002). The Third World slum is another comparable case to the *chengzhongcun*. In a way, slum problem is facing the developing world as a whole, although it has its own characteristics in different countries. Given the fact that most of the urbanisation will be happening in the developing world, it is highly suggested that China should share its experiences of both success and failure in urbanisation with other countries.

TROUBLED HISTORY, UNCERTAIN FUTURE

Ever since the city has gained its dominant position *vis a vis* the countryside, the relationship between the two has been punctuated with struggles. The German historian Oswald Spengler has linked the fate of the city with that of the Western civilization, "we cannot comprehend political and economic history at all unless we realize that the city, with its gradual detachment from and final bankrupting of the country, is the determinative form to which the course and sense of higher history generally conforms. *World history is city history*" (Spengler, 1927: 95, original emphasis in italic).

If the city represents the heights of human civilization, as so many scholars repeatedly asserted, then it is the time to question the divide between urban and rural. In modern history, the rebellion of the countryside against the city culminated with the socialist revolution. It is worth recalling the early 1920s optimism in Russia that "viewed the Revolution – the 'proletarian' revolution – as the triumph of the Russian village over the urban way of life" (Clark, 1985: 178). For a few decades, the cities of the socialist block were the antithesis to the Western urban world for its self-proclaimed mission of eliminating the divide between the city and the countryside. With the end of the Cold War thirty years ago, the utopian dream of creating an egalitarian, just, and transnational society is now stiff dead.

However, few would have anticipated that "the departure from the world stage not only of the Soviet system but also, at least as it seems at present, of the idea of socialism, occurred with a whimper rather than a bang" (Outhwaite & Ray, 2005: i). The dissolution of the Soviet Union was neither a direct result of military conflict (as in the case of colonial rule) nor irreversible internal collapse (as in the case of civil war), but rather boredom: the boredom of equality and homogeneity. The Soviet cities were conceived—as much as possible—as mere agglomerations of industrial production units and integrated reproduction processes of their labour force. Both economics and politics were ruled by redistribution. It would never be able to produce an urban lifestyle as envisioned by Louis Wirth, who defined urbanism as size, density, and heterogeneity. While the two first features applied to socialist cities, the third one was absent: complete submission of the city to industrial production, low levels of social inequalities imposed by planning, and urban growth constrained by planning objectives. Cooperation and obedience were the price paid for achieving livelihood security offered by the plan. It may have an appropriate size and it may have enough density, but it could never reconcile with heterogeneity. It is doubtful, too, whether the Soviet city was really a society of equality, and if so whether it is desirable, is the means legitimate, and finally whether it is sustainable. History has given us, at least to the last of these questions, a clear and plain answer. In this sense, Soviet urbanism was not urbanism.

NORMAL URBANISM

So far, this study on the *chengzhongcun* has been focused the situation in mainland China. The *chengzhongcun*, as has been noted, first emerged in the Pearl River Delta (PRD) in mid-1980s. There is nothing special or secret about the fact that many of the foreign direct investment (FDI) projects came to the mainland via Hong Kong, then a British colony. It is hardly surprising that, along with the influx of capital, cities in the PRD, particularly Shenzhen, also learnt from Hong Kong's experiences of urban development.

Back in November 1972, the Executive Council of the Hong Kong government promulgated the *New Territories Small House Policy*. Unlike the Hong Kong island and the Kowloon peninsula, the so-called New Territories were annexed to the Hong Kong colony in 1898 in a treaty between British and the Qing governments when the later leased it out for a duration of 99 years. So, strictly speaking, the New Territories were not colony. It was in this context that the *New Territories Small House Policy* recognizes the so-called "Ding Right" for "an indigenous villager to apply for permission to erect, for once in his lifetime, a small house on a suitable site within his own village" (Lands Department, The Government of the Hong Kong SAR, 2021).[1] These buildings were limited to

---

[1] For a general overview on the history and legal status of the Ding Right, see: Ng, T. (2016). Small House Policy. Research Office, Secretariat of the Legislative Council of the Hong Kong Special Administrative Region of the People's Republic of China. Available at: https://www.legco.gov.hk/research-publications/english/essentials-1516ise10-small-house-policy.htm [Accessed September 22, 2021].

three stories in height, and c. 210 square meters maximum in floor area. [Re-]Constructed in the villages surrounded by urban areas of one of the highest density, even if separated and scattered due to Hong Kong's mountainous topography, houses in these villages are sought after even by urbanites, including academic visitors in the Chinese University of Hong Kong.

Notwithstanding the institutional differences, it is hard not to observe the similarities between these villages and the *chengzhongcuns* just across the border in Shenzhen. Some of the villages in the New Territories were kept intact because the Hong Kong government needed the support of the residents for urban development on their agricultural land. And the rights to private and independent housing of the indigenous villagers were acknowledged and protected. So much so that in a city where housing shortage is chronicle, the right to housing is also the right to financial resource. Recently, this has lead Cliff Buddle, a correspondent of the South China Morning Post (SCMP), to put forth an analogy between the Small-house policy and the right to print money (Buddle, 2021). In the same vein, most of the native *chengzhongcun* residents that I have encountered during the visits and surveys showed little to no attachment or affection, let alone nostalgia for the lifestyle, to the village. In Deng Xiaoping's China, getting rich is glorious. There is little reason to turn down the offer of compensations in kind and/or in cash.

The Hong Kong SAR has the rule-of-law, a civil society, a free market economy, and consumerism. But is that how the future urbanism in mainland China looks like? The answer is probably no. But that is not the point. The point is to acknowledge the differences and yet see the similarities through the differences. It is helpful to keep in mind that it is always possible to go "back to beginnings in the cities" (Solinger, 1999). But getting urbanised is nothing special. Building brand new cities from scratches is nothing special either. There is nothing uniquely Chinese. People have been there (Fig. 7.1).

The rural–urban relationship has been a useful handle in approaching the fundamentals of China studies. David Faure and Liu Tao Tao observed that "what the educated Westerner might mean by 'city' or 'village' does not correspond to what the educated Chinese person means by *cheng* or *xiang*" (Faure & Liu, 2002: 2). Accordingly, Tang Wing-Shing devised "a more relevant concept of *cheng*-cum-*xiang* to capture the subtleties of the mutual embeddedness between *cheng* and *xiang* in China" (Tang, 2019a: 374).

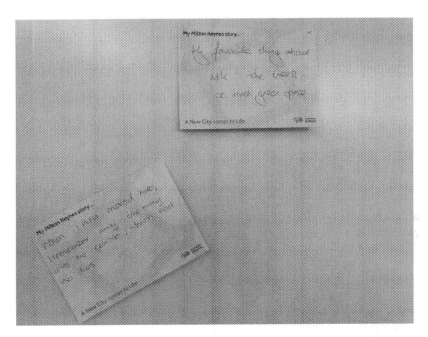

Fig. 7.1 Visitors' notes on the 50th anniversary of Milton Keynes (*Source* Photo taken by the author on January 10, 2017, Milton Keynes, United Kingdom)

It is not quite clear how that sounds in the ears of those readers who are not yet familiar with Chinese history and culture. There is a danger in overemphasizing the role of geography. Geography matters only if the geographically defined space corresponds to the mechanism that produces the city in the first place. In urban liberty, Robert Park observes that "[L]aw, of itself, could not, however, have made the craftsman free. An open market in which he might sell the products of his labor was a necessary incident of his freedom, and it was the application of the money economy to the relations of master and man that completed the emancipation of the serf" (Park, 1984: 12. First published in 1925).

I believe Faure had dramatised his critique on Max Weber in the same work so as to make a case for his own research agenda. But that critique was rather misplaced. What is at stake isn't the administrative status of a given town or city, but rather whether it is governed as a city and foster urbanism. To his questions, namely "it is not clear if the argument states that the urban environment served as a necessary or an incidental cradle for capitalism," and that "nothing in the argument has to suggest that business institutions must necessarily be invented in towns rather than, say, in the countryside, or that they must be invented by merchants rather than, say, farmers" (Faure, 2002: 59), we may firmly respond by saying: Yes, it takes the city to do the trick.

The problem is, and I am writing from a Chinese perspective, that for too long industrialisation and urbanisation have been portrayed in a positive light in China and, possibly, other developing countries. This view has been institutionalised with a undisguised urban bias. Historically, the tensions between the urban and the rural, and between the city and the state, have fueled social revolutions. In this post-revolutionary age, and as China is getting more urbanised than ever, the way ahead probably starts by taking urbanism as it is.

References

Buddle, C. (2021, January 16). Small-house policy has become a right to print money. *The South China Morning Post*. Available at: https://www.scmp.com/comment/opinion/article/3118027/small-house-policy-has-become-right-print-money [Accessed September 22, 2021].

Clark, K. (1985). The city versus the countryside in Soviet Peasant literature of the twenties: A duel of Utopias. In A. Gleason, P. Kenez, & R. Stites (Eds.), *Bolshevik culture: Experiment and order in the Russian Revolution* (pp. 175–189). Indiana University Press.

Faure, D. (2002). What Weber did not know: Towns and economic development in Ming and Qing China. In D. Faure & T. T. Liu (Eds.), *Town and country in China: Identity and perception* (pp. 58–84). Palgrave.

Faure, D., & Liu, T. T. (2002). Introduction. In D. Faure & T. T. Liu (Eds.), *Town and country in China: Identity and perception* (pp. 1–16). Palgrave.

Gans, H. J. (1982). *The Levittowners: Ways of life and politics in a new suburban community* (3rd edition). First published in 1967. Columbia University Press.

Gans, H. J. (1990). Deconstructing the underclass The term's dangers as a planning concept. *Journal of the American Planning Association, 56*(3), 271–277. https://doi.org/10.1080/01944369008975772

Gans, H. J. (2002). Uses and misuses of concepts in American social science research: Variations on Loïc Wacquant's theme of 'three pernicious premises in the study of the American Ghetto'. *International Journal of Urban and Regional Research, 21*(3), 504–507. https://doi.org/10.1111/1468-2427.00093

Kesteloot, C. (2004). *The Chinese city as a geological metaphor: A framework for analysis*. In Conference Proceedings of the International Symposium on "Urban settlements in the frontier zones under the Chinese civilization", Nara Women's University, Japan, pp.104–114.

Lands Department, The Government of the Hong Kong SAR. (2021). *Village houses in the new territories*. Available at: https://www.landsd.gov.hk/en/land-disposal-transaction/village-houses-NT.html [Accessed September 22, 2021].

Mote, F. (1977). The transformation of Nanking, 1350–1400. In W. Skinner (Ed.), *The city in late imperial China* (pp. 102–105). Stanford University Press.

Outhwaite, W., & Ray, L. (2005). *Social theory and post-communism*. Blackwell.

Park, R. E. (1984). The city: Suggestions for the investigation of human behavior in the urban environment. In R. E. Park, E. W. Burgess, & R. D. McKenzie (Eds.), *The city* (pp. 1–46). University of Chicago Press.

Solinger, D. J. (1999). *Contesting citizenship in urban China: Peasant migrants, the state and the logic of the market*. University of California Press.

Spengler, O. (1927). *The decline of the West: Form and actuality*. Alfred A. Knopf.

Tang, W. S. (2019a). Introduction: Urban China research is dead, long live urban China research. *Eurasian Geography and Economics, 60*(4), 369–375. https://doi.org/10.1080/15387216.2019.1699434

Tang, W. S. (2019b). Town-country relations in China: Back to basics. *Eurasian Geography and Economics, 60*(4), 455–485. https://doi.org/10.1080/15387216.2019.1686407

APPENDIX

Social Integration and Urban Recognition of Chengzhongcun Residents (Shanghai)[1]

1. Personal information

1.1 Age ____			1.2 Ethnicity ____		
1.3 Gender	Male	( )	**1.4** Education	Primary school or below	( )
	Female	( )		Middle schools	( )
				University or above	( )

2. Housing conditions

2.1 How long have you been living here? _____ years					
2.2 In total, your house consists of _____ rooms, in total _____ sq. meters. There are _____ people living inside.					
2.3 Property Ownership	Private	( )	**2.4** Use Right	Private owned	( )
	Public	( )		Private rent	( )
	Not sure	( )		Pubic rent	( )
				Others	please specify: _____

3. Do you have your own kitchen in your house

Yes	( )	No	( )

[1] Originally in Chinese with privacy and data protection statements.

4. Is your kitchen and your bedroom the same room

Yes	( )	No	( )

5. Is your water tap a public one

Yes	( )	No	( )

6. Do you have your own toilet in your house

Yes	( )	No	( )

7. Citizenship

7.1 *Hukou* status	Non- Shanghai rural	( )
	Non- Shanghai urban	( )
	Shanghai rural	( )
	Shanghai urban	( )
7.2 Are you a 1st. generation migrant	Yes	( )
	No	( )
7.3 Have you ever changed your *hukou* status	Yes	( )
	No	( )

8. Employment

8.1 Please choose your employment status	Long term job	( )
	Short term job	( )
	Non-employment, e.g. student	( )
	Un-employed	( )
	Retired	( )
8.2 Employment type	Public employee	( )
	Managerial or technical staff	( )
	Contracted laborer	( )
	Self-employed	( )
	Others please specify: _____	
8.3 Monthly income interval _____ (CNY)	1000 or below	( )
	1000 - 2000	( )
	2000 - 3000	( )
	3000 - 4000	( )
	4000 or above	( )

9. Regarding the prospects of settling down and getting integrated into the city, which are the most feasible channels? And which ones are the obstacles? Pick THREE from the options and write it down in a descending order:

	9.1 Channels			9.2 Obstacles
1	Long term employment		1	Education level
2	Admission to higher education		2	Income level
3	Purchasing a house		3	*Hukou*
4	Marriage		4	Difference of lifestyles
5	Relocation through redevelopment		5	Difference of languages
6	Join the army		6	Urban discrimination
7	Others		7	Others
	Your answer here _____			Your answer here _____

10. In the diagrams (see below) we use gray gradients to indicate the degrees of urbanisation.

    Q: Which one do you think best capture the situation of the chengzhongcun?

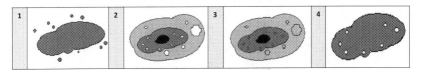

    Your answer here: _____

11. How much do you (dis-)agree with these statements?

		Strongly con	Con	Not sure	Pro	Strongly pro
1.	The *chengzhongcun* is different from the city outside					
2.	I am used to the urban lifestyle					
3.	The more urbanized, the higher living standard					
4.	The more urbanized, the more happiness					
5.	The *chengzhongcun* is essentially urban					
6.	The *chengzhongcun* is essentially rural					
7.	Redevelopment of the *chengzhongcun* benefits me					
8.	I live here because I can't get integrated to the city					
9.	This place should be preserved from redevelopment					
10.	Urbanization should be lead by the government					
11.	Urbanization should be lead by the people					
12.	Living in the *chengzhongcun* helped me to urbanize					
13.	I want to change my *hukou* if it is possible					
14.	The *chengzhongcun* is over-crowded					
15.	The redevelopment will force me to relocate					
16.	I would like to move out as soon as I can					
17.	Rural life is better than in the city					
18.	I didn't benefit from urbanization					
19.	*chengzhongcun* redevelopment destroys community					
20.	The *chengzhongcun* helped my family to urbanize					
21.	EXPO 2010 /Grand Construction is good to the city					
22.	The *chengzhongcun* lacks a sense of neighborhood					
23.	The people is under-represented in redevelopment					
24.	I would like to stay here as long as I can					
25.	The *chengzhongcun* is more livable than the city					

———————————— End of the questionnaire ————————

INDEX

Printed in the United States
by Baker & Taylor Publisher Services